# Study Guide

*for*

# *Pinel*

# BIOPSYCHOLOGY

## *Fourth Edition*

Michael J. Mana
*Western Washington University*

John P.J. Pinel
*University of British Colombia*

Allyn and Bacon
Boston   London   Toronto   Sydney   Tokyo   Singapore

ISBN 0-205-28993-2

Printed in the United States of America

10 9 8 7 6 5 4 3 2 1   03 02 01 00 99

# TABLE OF CONTENTS

|  |  |  |
|---|---|---|
| | Introduction | 1 |
| Chapter 1: | Biopsychology as a Neuroscience | 5 |
| Chapter 2: | Evolution, Genetics, and Experience: Asking the Right Questions About the Biology of Behavior | 17 |
| Chapter 3: | The Anatomy of the Nervous System | 33 |
| Chapter 4: | Neural Conduction and Synaptic Transmission | 47 |
| Chapter 5: | What Biopsychologists Do: The Research Methods of Biopsychology | 64 |
| Chapter 6: | Human Brain Damage and Animal Models | 79 |
| Chapter 7: | The Visual System: From Eye to Cortex | 94 |
| Chapter 8: | Mechanisms of Perception, Conscious Awareness, and Attention | 111 |
| Chapter 9: | The Sensorimotor System | 129 |
| Chapter 10: | The Biopsychology of Eating and Drinking | 146 |
| Chapter 11: | Hormones and Sex | 170 |
| Chapter 12: | Sleep, Dreaming, and Circadian Rhythms | 191 |
| Chapter 13: | Drug Addiction and Reward Circuits in the Brain | 210 |
| Chapter 14: | Memory and Amnesia | 231 |
| Chapter 15: | Neuroplasticity: Development, Learning, and Recovery from Brain Damage | 250 |
| Chapter 16: | Lateralization, Language, and the Split Brain | 270 |
| Chapter 17: | The Biopsychology of Emotion, Stress and Mental Illness | 289 |

# INTRODUCTION

Welcome! This is the study guide for the fourth edition of BIOPSYCHOLOGY, and we hope that our efforts will help you to improve your grades, increase your understanding of BIOPSYCHOLOGY, and stimulate your interest this area of scientific study. The design of the study guide is based on the following four principles of good study habits:

**Active Studying:** Studying is far more effective when it is active. Many students prepare for examinations by simply reading the assigned material over and over, but such attempts to passively absorb material are not very productive. Studies have repeatedly shown that the acquisition, comprehension, and retention of knowledge are all better when a student actively engages the material under study. We hope to help you in this endeavor of active learning, by encouraging you to think about the critical issues in each chapter and then to write out answers to key essay questions.

**Bidirectional Studying:** In order to be fully prepared, a student must study bidirectionally. Many students actively prepare for examinations by repeatedly reviewing a set of study questions. Because most questions about specific points can be posed in two opposite ways, students who study in this manner may be unable to answer questions about the points that they have studied if they are posed in the opposite way. For example, a student who can successfully answer the question, "Who is John Pinel?" may not be able to answer the question, "Who is the author of Biopsychology?". The Jeopardy section of each chapter in this study guide specifically focuses on bidirectional study habits.

**Multiple-level Studying:** Effective study focuses on different levels of detail. Some students study by reviewing details while others study by thinking about general concepts and issues. However, in neither of these cases does the student gain a complete grasp of the material, and in neither case is the student prepared to write an examination that includes a variety of different kinds of test items. In order to be fully prepared, it is necessary to study both detail and general concepts and issues.

**Formal Pretesting:** The best way for a student to assess the progress of her or his studying is to write a practice examination. The results of a practice examination written under self-imposed examination conditions a day or two before a scheduled examination will indicate the areas that require special last-minute review. Each chapter in this study guide contains a full-length practice examination, complete with an answer key, that is similar to the ones that we have used in our own classes.

**There Are Three Sections in Each Chapter of This Study Guide**

There are 17 chapters in this study guide, each of which is associated with one of the 17 chapters of BIOPSYCHOLOGY. Each chapter of this study guide includes the following three sections.

## Section I: Jeopardy Study Items

For the lack of a more original alternative, we have named the first items in each chapter of the study guide "Jeopardy Study Items" after Jeopardy, the popular television quiz show. This quiz show differs from other quiz shows in that the contestants are given the answers and are asked to come up with the correct questions. The jeopardy items in each chapter are arranged in two columns, with the questions in the left column and the answers in the right. Sometimes there is nothing in the space to the right of a question, and your task is to fill the space with the correct answer; sometimes there is nothing in the space to the left of an answer, and your task is to fill the space with the correct question. In order to insure that your answers and questions are correct, you should use your text to complete these items. When you have completed this section, you will have a series of questions and answers that summarize the key points in each chapter. Moreover, they will be conveniently arranged on the page so that you can readily practice bidirectional studying: Cover the right column and practice anticipating the correct answers to each question, and then cover the left column and practice anticipating the correct questions to each answer.

## Section II: Essay Study Questions

The purpose of the essay study questions is to make sure that you do not fail to see the forest for the trees; their purpose is to focus your attention on general principles, concepts, and issues. The essay study questions cover much of the same material as do the jeopardy study items, but they do so at a more general, integrative level of analysis.

## Section III: Practice Examination

In the third and last section of each chapter is a practice examination, which is intended to help you assess the progress of your studying. Each practice examination is composed of several kinds of questions: multiple-choice questions, fill-in-the-blanks questions, modified true-false questions, short-answer questions, and diagram questions. After writing each practice examination, mark it -- the answers are at the end of each chapter -- and use your performance to plan the final stages of your studying.

**How to Use This Study Guide To Prepare for an Examination**

The recommended method for using this study guide involves the following eight steps:

1.  Read the assigned chapter from BIOPSYCHOLOGY. Underline particularly important or difficult parts as you read.

2.  Using BIOPSYCHOLOGY, complete the jeopardy study items in the appropriate chapter of the study guide. These items are arranged in the order in which they appear in the text to make it easy for you to complete them.

3.  Study the jeopardy study items by covering up the left half of each page and thinking through the correct answer to each covered question. Then, cover the right half of each page and think through the correct question for every covered answer. Repeat until your performance is error free. Each time that you fail to correctly anticipate a question or answer, put an asterisk next to it so that you can focus on these items during the final phases of your studying.

4.  Using BIOPSYCHOLOGY, write the outline of your best answer to each essay study question. Memorize each outline. Put an asterisk next to any essay question that gives you a problem.

5.  Read through the assigned chapter again, focusing on what you have previously underlined. Before you turn a page, try to anticipate and think through all of the underlined points on the next page. Place an asterisk next to any point that you have trouble anticipating.

6.  Study the list of key words at the end of the chapter in BIOPSYCHOLOGY. Practice bidirectional studying until you can go from term to definition and from definition to term without making an error. Each time that you miss a term or definition, put an asterisk next to it.

7.  Write the appropriate practice examination in this study guide at least 24 hours before you are scheduled to write your formal examination. Grade your practice examination by referring to the correct answers that follow it. Place an asterisk next to each item that you get wrong.

8.  On the basis of your performance on the practice examination, plan the final phases of your studying. At some point during the last day of preparation, make sure that you can respond correctly to each point with an asterisk next to it.

Dear Student:

I do hope that this study guide will make BIOPSYCHOLOGY a more worthwhile and enjoyable experience for you, but I am not going to wish you good luck in your quest for knowledge and high grades. If you put this study guide to good use, you will not need good luck.

If you have any comments, suggestions, or questions about this study guide or about BIOPSYCHOLOGY, please write to me at the Department of Psychology, 2136 West Mall, University of British Columbia, Vancouver, B.C., Canada V6T 1Z4.

Cordially,

John Pinel

Greetings!

I am happy to once again be involved with the study guide for the fourth edition of BIOPSYCHOLOGY. We have included many new questions in this fourth edition of the study guide. In addition, previous users have regularly suggested that more diagrams would be greatly appreciated...in response, you will find diagram-type study questions included with almost every chapter in this edition of the study guide. You will recognize some of these diagrams from the chapters of BIOPSYCHOLOGY. Many others are from the book *A Colorful Introduction to the Anatomy of the Human Brain,* by John P.J. Pinel and Maggie Edwards (Allyn and Bacon, 1998; ISBN 0-205-16299-1); I highly recommend this book to anyone interested in knowing more about functional neuroanatomy.

When all is said and done, I sincerely hope that this study guide increases your understanding of the material presented in BIOPSYCHOLOGY while it nurtures your excitement for this captivating field of study. If you have any questions or comments feel free to contact me. You can write me at the Department of Psychology, Miller Hall, Western Washington University, Bellingham, WA, 98226. Better yet, e-me at MIKE.MANA@WWU.EDU or drop me a line through the new website for BIOPSYCHOLOGY, which you can find at:

*http://www.abacon.com/pinel*

The website for BIOPSYCHOLOGY should prove to be another valuable study resource for you; it includes hundreds of links that complement the material explored in each chapter of BIOPSYCHOLOGY, a Questions-&-Answers area that I will participate in called *"Questions? Comments? Confusion?,* and a *"Hot Topics"* area focusing on the latest news and research in the behavioral and brain sciences. Check it out, and let us know what you think!

All the Best,

---

# Chapter 1

# BIOPSYCHOLOGY AS A NEUROSCIENCE

---

I.     **Jeopardy Study Items**

*With reference to Chapter 1 of BIOPSYCHOLOGY, write the correct answer to each of the following questions and the correct question for each of the following answers.*

1. What is neuroscience?

2. Who was Jimmie G.?

3.                                                          A: This is the scientific study of the nervous system.

4. What is biopsychology?

5. Who was D.O. Hebb?

6.  What unique contribution did Hebb make to the study
    of the biological bases of behavior?

7.  Biopsychology is greatly influenced by six other subdisciplines of neuroscience.  Define each of these
    subdisciplines; when you are provided with a definition, provide the name of the subdiscipline.  (p. 5)

    a.  neuroanatomy

    b.                              A: This is the study of the interactions of the nervous system
                                    with the endocrine glands and the hormones they release.

    c.  neurochemistry

    d.                              A: This is the study of nervous system disorders.

    e.  neuropharmacology

    f.                              A: This is the study of the functions and activities of the
                                    nervous system.

8.  What are 3 advantages that human subjects have
    over nonhuman subjects in biopsychological
    research?

9.  Why does neuroscientific research often focus on
    nonhuman animals?

10. What is the difference between a within-subjects design
    and a between-subjects design?

11. Define or identify the following three kinds of experimental variables.

    a.    independent variable

    b.                       A: This is the variable measured by the experimenter.

    c.    confounded variable

12.                        A: This refers to the observation that sexually fatigued animals will often recommence copulation if a new sex partner is provided.

13. Define or name the following three types of research.

    a.    experiment

    b.                       A: This is a study in which subjects are exposed to conditions of interest in real-world conditions

    c.                       A: This is the study of a single subject, and is often limited in its generalizability.

14. What is the difference between pure research and applied research?

15. Why do many scientists believe that pure research will ultimately provide more practical benefit than applied research?

16. Define or name the following six divisions of biopsychology.

   a.  physiological psychology


   b.                                    A: This is the study of effects of drugs on behavior and how
                                         they are mediated by the nervous system.


   c.  neuropsychology


   d.                                    A: This is the study of the relationship between physiological
                                         processes and psychological processes in humans.

   e.  cognitive neuroscience


   f.                                    A: This is the study of the evolution, genetics, and
                                         adaptiveness of behavior, often by using the comparative
                                         method.



17.                                      A: This is the study of an animal's behavior in its natural
                                         environment.


18. Define the concept of "converging operations".



19.                                      A: This is the method that scientists use to study the
                                         unobservable.



20. What two features of biopsychological research make it
    particularly susceptible to error?



21. "To know where you're going, you must know where
    you've been!". Why is it important to be aware of
    previous errors in biopsychological research?

22. What is the most reasonable interpretation of Delgado's charging-bull demonstration?

23.                                              A: This is the idea that when several explanations exist for an observation, precedence should be given to the simplest one.

24. What is a prefrontal lobotomy?

25. Who were Moniz, Lima and Freeman?

26. Who was Becky, and what is her claim to fame in the field of biopsychology?

27. What were some of the undesirable side effects of the prefrontal lobotomy procedure?

---

**Once you have completed the jeopardy study items, study them. Practice bidirectional studying; make sure that you know the correct answer to every question and the correct question for every answer.**

## II.    Essay Study Questions

*Using Chapter 1 of BIOPSYCHOLOGY, prepare an outline for each of the following essay questions.*

1.  In the *Organization of Behavior,* Hebb combined research on animals and humans with clinical and day-to-day observations to support his theory that psychological phenomena could be produced by the activity of the brain.  How is this eclectic approach reflected in current biopsychological inquiry?

2.  How do biopsychologists use observational methods to study unobservable phenomena?  Give an example.

3. Compare and contrast experiments, quasiexperimental studies, and case studies.

4. Compare and contrast the six divisions of biopsychology. Include a description of the key experimental approach and techniques used in each area.

5. Describe the case of caudate stimulation and the charging bull. What does this case teach us about good and bad science?

6. Describe the development of prefrontal lobotomy as a treatment for psychological dysfunction. What lessons does this episode teach us about good science and bad science?

> **When you have answered the essay study questions, memorize your outlines to prepare for your upcoming examination.**

## III. Practice Examination

*After completing most of your studying of Chapter 1, but at least 24 hours before your formal examination, complete the following practice examination.*

**A. Multiple-Choice Section.** Circle the correct answer for each question; *REMEMBER that some questions may have more than one correct answer.*

1. Biopsychology can be considered to be a division of:

    a. physiological psychology.
    b. neuroscience.
    c. neuroanatomy.
    d. neurophysiology.

2. According to the text, who played a major role in the emergence of biopsychology as a discipline?

    a. Lashley
    b. Moniz
    c. Hebb
    d. Sperry

3. Korsakoff's syndrome is:

    a. characterized by severe memory loss.
    b. caused by surgical excision of the frontal lobes.
    c. associated with amorality, lack of foresight and emotional unresponsiveness.
    d. caused by a thiamin (vitamin B1) deficiency.

4. Cognitive neuroscience is:

    a. the youngest division of biopsychology.
    b. concerned with the relation between physiological activity and psychological processes in human subjects.
    c. concerned with the neural bases of cognition.
    d. often concerned with functional brain imaging while subjects are engaged in a particular activity.

5. A comparison between the performance of alcoholics and that of age-matched nonalcoholics on a test of memory would qualify as:

    a. a quasiexperimental study.
    b. an experiment.
    c. a case study.
    d. a within-subject study.

6. Biopsychological research aimed at developing better psychotherapeutic drugs is:

    a. applied research.
    b. psychopharmacological research.
    c. pure research.
    d. rarely done with nonhuman subjects.

7. The effects of electrical brain stimulation on the behavior of rats would most likely be studied by a:

    a. comparative psychologist.
    b. psychopharmacologist.
    c. psychophysiologist.
    d. physiological psychologist

8. The study of the integrated behavior of different species of animals describes the subdiscipline of:

    a. psychobiology
    b. comparative psychology
    c. neuropsychology
    d. psychopharmacology

9. Merton was both the experimenter and the subject in a classic experiment on eye movement. Merton's experiment was an example of:

    a. a quasiexperiment.
    b. the use of scientific inference in biopsychological research
    c. applied biopsychological research.
    d. a case study.

10. Delgado's demonstration that caudate stimulation prevented the charge of a raging bull supports the idea that:

    a. he had located the taming center of the bull's brain.
    b. he had activated a neural pathway controlling movement.
    c. he had a flair for the dramatic, if not the scientific method.
    d. caudate stimulation could be used to calm human psychopaths.

11. Prefrontal lobotomy was a surgical treatment:

    a. intended as a treatment for mental illness.
    b. in which electrodes were implanted into the brain.
    c. involving large bilateral lesions of the prefrontal lobes.
    d. with considerable therapeutic success.

**B. Modified True-False and Fill-in-the Blank Section.** If the statement is true, write TRUE in the blank provided. If the statement is false, write FALSE as well as the word or words that will make the statement true if they replaced the highlighted word or words in the original statement. If the statement is incomplete, write the word or words that will complete it.

1. **True or False:** <u>Mice</u> are the most common nonhuman subjects in biopsychology experiments.

     **A:** _____

2. By definition, a confounded variable is an unintended difference between experimental conditions that can affect the _____ variable.

3. In their well-controlled study, Lester and Gorzalka (1988) demonstrated that the Coolidge effect is not restricted to _____.

4. **True or False:** The amnesiac effect of alcohol abuse results, to a large degree, from **<u>alcohol-induced neurotoxicity.</u>**

     **A:** _____

5. Neuropsychology is largely focused on the effects of damage to _____ on human behavior.

6. The measure of brain activity most often recorded by psychophysiologists is the scalp _____.

7. Progress is most rapid when different research approaches are brought to bear on the same problem. This approach is called _____.

8. Scientists find out about unobservable phenomena by drawing scientific _____ from events that they can observe.

9. **True or False:** **<u>Comparative psychology</u>** focuses on the neural bases of higher intellectual processes such as thought, memory, or attention.

     **A:** _____

10. The disaster of _____ as a therapeutic form of psychosurgery emphasizes the need to carefully evaluate the consequences of such procedures on the first patients to receive such an operation.

**C. Short Answer Section.** In no more than 5 sentences, answer each of the following questions.

1. Biopsychology often takes an integrative, comparative approach to the study of brain/behavior relations. Discuss the merits of this type of research.

2. Chapter 1 of BIOPSYCHOLOGY concludes with two examples of bad science: one about prefrontal lobotomy and the other about raging bulls. For each "rule of good research" provided below, describe how each example described in Chapter 1 violates the qualities of good scientific protocol.

   a. In interpreting behavior, Morgan's Canon should always be heeded.

   b. Researchers should be especially cautious when involved in the objective evaluation of their own efforts.

   c. It is important to test any putative therapeutic procedure on a variety of species before using it as a treatment for human disorders.

3. The use of nonhuman subjects instead of human subjects has several advantages in biopsychological research; describe each of the advantages.

Chapter 1

> **Mark your answers to the practice examination; the correct answers follow.  On the basis of your performance, plan the final stages of your studying.**

**Answers to Practice Examination**

### A. Multiple Choice Section

1. b
2. c
3. a, d
4. a, c, d
5. a
6. a, b

7. d
8. b
9. b, d
10. b
11. a, c

### B. Modified True/False and Fill-in-the-Blank Section

1. False; rats
2. dependent
3. males
4. False; a thiamin deficiency
5. the cerebral cortex

6. EEG
7. converging operations
8. inferences
9. False; Cognitive neuroscience
10. prefrontal lobotomy

### C. Short Answer Section

1. Mention that integrative research takes advantage of the strength of multiple methods and perspectives; that scientific progress is most rapid when different approaches are focused on a single problem; that a comparative approach can take advantage of the strengths of both human and nonhuman research.

2. a) Mention Morgan's Canon, and how in each example the simplest explanation for the data was ignored for an explanation that the experimenters wanted to believe to be true.

   b) Mention the lack of objectivity that was implicit in the conclusions that each group of researchers reached about their work.

   c) Mention the dangers in rushing a new procedure into use as a therapeutic tool before it is thoroughly tested.

3. Mention the similarities between the brains of human and nonhuman species; the benefits of a comparative approach to the study of behavior; the ethical considerations that restrict many kinds of experimentation on human beings.

---

# Chapter 2

## EVOLUTION, GENETICS, AND EXPERIENCE: ASKING THE RIGHT QUESTIONS ABOUT THE BIOLOGY OF BEHAVIOR

---

## I.    Jeopardy Study Items

*With reference to Chapter 2 of BIOPSYCHOLOGY, write the correct answer to each of the following questions and the correct question for each of the following answers*

1.  What is a Zeitgeist?

2.                                          A: This idea grew out of a seventeenth-century conflict between science and the Roman church.

3.  What was Cartesian dualism, and what effect did it have on the scientific study of behavior?

4.                                          A: This is often referred to as the *nature-nurture* debate.

5.                                          A: He was the father of *behaviorism.*

6.  Describe two kinds of evidence that contradict physiological-or-psychological thinking about behavior.

7.                                          A: This is a branch of the behavioral sciences that focuses on the study of instinctive behaviors.

8.  What is asomatognosia?

9.  Why is evidence that chimpanzees are self-aware significant to the study of the mind?

10. Why is the nature-or-nurture controversy fundamentally flawed when studying the biological bases of behavior?

11. All behavior is the product of interactions among three factors. What are they?

12. What three kinds of evidence did Darwin offer to support his theory of evolution?

13.                                        A: This is the process by which new species develop from preexisting species.

14. What is natural selection?

15. What is the relationship between the terms *species* and *conspecific?*

16. What role does social dominance play in evolution?

17. How do courtship displays promote the evolution of new species?

18.    A: This is the ability of an organism to survive and contribute its genes to the next generation.

19.    What is the definition of a *chordate?*

20.    A: This bony structure may have evolved to protect the dorsal nerve chord.

21.    How and why did land-dwelling vertebrates evolve from fishes?

22.    What 2 key evolutionary changes were first seen in reptiles?

23.    What is a mammal?

24.    What developmental alteration allows mammals the opportunity for more complex programs of development to unfold?

25.    A: This order of primates includes prosimians, new-world monkeys, old-world monkeys, apes, and hominids.

26.    A: This was *Homo erectus.*

27.    How old is the species *Homo sapiens?*

28.                                        A: These features include a big brain, an upright posture and a workable, opposing thumb.

29. What is the definition of homologous evolutionary structures?

30.                                        A: This refers to the evolution of similar solutions to the same environmental demands by unrelated species.

31. What evidence suggests that brain size is not a good measure of intellectual capacity?

32. Why is it better to consider the evolution of the brain stem and cerebrum independently?

33.                                        A: These are folds on the cerebral surface that greatly increase the volume of the cerebral cortex.

34.                                        A: This approach emphasizes the study of behavioral and neural mechanisms in terms of adaptation and the environmental pressures that led to their evolution.

35. Describe the *comparative approach* to the study of brain/behavior relations.

36. What two key decisions led to Mendel's success in his research on inheritance in pea plants?

37. What is the difference between genotype and phenotype?

38. What is a gene?

39.                                              A: These are the thread-like structures in the nucleus that
                                                 contain a cell's genes.

40. Describe the key difference between meiosis and mitosis.

41. Why is the phenomenon of "crossing over" important?

42.                                              A: These chromosomes do not come in matched pairs

43. Why do recessive sex-linked traits such as color
    blindness occur more often in males?

44.                                              A: This is an accidental alteration in an individual gene.

45. How does DNA self-duplicate?

46.                                              A: These control gene expression so that different kinds of
                                                 cells can develop. .

47. What is the Human Genome Project?

48. Describe 2 ways that the Human Genome Project is of
    interest to behavioral scientists.

49. Why was the "cross fostering" control procedure
    important to Tryon's work?

50. What important caveat should you keep in mind when assessing studies of selective breeding?

51.                                    A: This disorder results from a single gene mutation that prevents the conversion of phenylalanine to tyrosine.

52.                                    A: This is the period of life during which a particular experience must occur for it to have a significant impact on development.

53. Describe the two common patterns of song acquisition and retention in songbirds.

54. Why is the seasonal change in the neural structures that underlie birdsong in the canary so remarkable?

55.                                    A: This describes siblings with an identical birthdate who developed from two zygotes.

56.                                    A: This describes the proportion of variability in a particular trait, in a particular study, that resulted from the genetic variation in that study.

57. How do genetic differences promote psychological differences?

**Once you have completed the jeopardy study items, study them. Practice bidirectional studying; make sure that you know the correct answer to every question and the correct question for every answer.**

## II.  Essay Study Questions

*Using Chapter 2 of BIOPSYCHOLOGY, write an outline to answer to each of the following essay study questions.*

1. People tend to think about the biology of behavior in terms of two dichotomies.  What are they, and what is wrong with these ways of thinking?

2. Describe the three-factor model that describes how many contemporary biopsychologists think about the biology of behavior.  Provide an example of this model.

3. *"Bigger is better"*.  Discuss this statement within the context of the evolution of the human brain.  Include a specific example in which this statement accurately describes the evolution of the human brain and an example illustrating the limits of this statement in the study of brain/behavior relations.

4. Describe the theory that Mendel developed to explain the results of his classic experiments on inheritance in pea plants.

5. *"The completion of the Human Genome Project will complete our understanding of the biological bases of behavior."* What is the key problem with this statement? Provide a more accurate assessment of the impact that the Human Genome Project will have on our understanding of brain/behavior relations.

6. Describe how Tryon's research on maze-dull and maze-bright rats undermined the idea that behavior is largely the result of experience. How would the results of the Minnesota Study of Twins Reared Apart also challenge this idea?

7. Describe the 2 main patterns of song acquisition and production in songbirds. Include a description of the key anatomical structures involved in song production, and a comparison of age-limited versus open-ended learners.

8. *"Behavioral capacities are the product of an interaction between genetics and experience"*. Discuss this idea with reference to maze-bright and maze-dull rats, the development of bird song, and the Minnesota Study of Twins Reared Apart.

9. What is the key difference between the development of individuals and the development of differences between individuals?

When you have answered the essay study questions, memorize your outlines to prepare for your upcoming examination

## III.    Practice Examination

*After completing most of your studying of Chapter 2, but at least 24 hours before your formal examination, complete the following practice examination.*

**A. Multiple-Choice Section.** Circle the correct answer for each question; *REMEMBER that some questions may have more than one correct answer.*

1. Gallup studied the self-awareness of chimpanzees by studying their reactions to:

    a. their images in a mirror.
    b. odorless red dots that had been painted on their eyebrow ridges while they were anesthetized.
    c. photographs of conspecifics.
    d. their interactions with one another.

2. According to Darwin, evolution is a product of:

    a. linkage.
    b. natural selection.
    c. crossing over.
    d. aggressive display.

3. According to the text, which of the following behaviors encourages the evolution of new species?

    a. courtship display
    b. social dominance
    c. aggressive behavior
    d. defensive behavior

4. Research has shown that canaries are:

    a. *age-limited* learners of their song repertoires.
    b. *open-ended* learners of their song repertoires.
    c. particularly effective in learning songs that they hear when they are between 10 and 50 days of age.
    d. able to return to a state of plastic song production at the end of each summer.

5. The canary song circuit is remarkable because:

    a. the left descending motor circuit is more important than the right descending motor circuit.
    b. the high vocal center is larger in females than males.
    c. the neural substrates underlying song production double in size each spring.
    d. the increase in the size of the neural substrates underlying song production reflects an increase in the size of existing neurons in these areas.

6. Cartesian dualism marked a critical point in the study of brain-behavior relations because:

    a. it gave one part of the universe to science and the other part to the Church.
    b. it separated the physical function of the body from the function of the mind.
    c. it suggested that the mind was a suitable subject for scientific investigation.
    d. it resolved the conflict between scientific knowledge and Church dogma that existed during the Renaissance.

7. In his monumental work *The Origin of Species,* Charles Darwin:

    a. was the first to propose that new species evolve from preexisting species.
    b. initiated the modern science of biology.
    c. was the first to suggest how evolution occurs.
    d. explained the role of Mendelian genetics in evolution.

8. As far as we can tell, the first hominids to produce works of art were:

    a. Cro-Magnons.
    b. Neanderthals.
    c. Homo sapiens.
    d. the Grateful Dead.

9. In selective breeding experiments, the possibility that behavioral characteristics are being transmitted from parent to offspring through learning is controlled for by:

    a. restricting the experiment to subjects of just one sex.
    b. using a cross-fostering procedure.
    c. restricting such research to the study of twins.
    d. raising the subjects in an enriched environment.

10. Sex-linked traits are:

    a. the product of chromosomes that do not come in matched pairs.
    b. almost always controlled by the Y chromosome.
    c. often more common in males if they are due to a recessive gene.
    d. controlled by genes on the sex chromosomes.

11. The control of gene expression is:

    a. under the control of operator genes.
    b. regulated by DNA-binding proteins.
    c. not sensitive to the environment that an organism exists in.
    d. important to the way a cell develops and then functions once it has reached maturity.

12. According to research such as the Minnesota Twins study, identical twins are:

    a. similar in intelligence and personality only if they were raised together.
    b. similar in both intelligence and personality regardless of whether or not they were raised together.
    c. so similar that the results proved that intelligence and personality are inherited traits.
    d. similar in every psychological trait that the researchers chose to study.

Chapter 2

**B. Modified True-False and Fill-in-the Blank Section.** If the statement is true, write TRUE in the blank provided. If the statement is false, write FALSE as well as the word or words that will make the statement true if they replaced the highlighted word or words in the original statement. If the statement is incomplete, write the word or words that will complete it.

1. The first mammals were egg-laying reptiles with _____ glands.

2. Mendel's experiments succeeded because he studied _dichotomos_ traits and _true breeding_ lines.

3. **True or False:** **Twin studies** provide an estimate of the proportion of variability occurring in a particular trait in a particular study that resulted from the genetic variation in that study.

    A: _____

4. Mitochondrial DNA is inherited from one's _____; its relatively constant

    rate of _____ allows scientists to use is as an evolutionary clock.

5. The hormone _____ has been implicated in the annual cycle of death and growth of song-circuit neurons.

6. **True or False:** Gametes are produced by **mitosis;** all other body cells are produced by the process of **meiosis.**

    A: _____

7. _____ are the closest living relatives of human beings; about _____ % of

    the genetic material is identical in these two species.

8. A _structural_ gene contains the information necessary for the synthesis of a single protein.

9. Diamond's finding that PKU children on special diets perform poorly on a variety of cognitive tests suggest

    that these children still suffer from brain damage; based on the types of deficits she saw, this damage is likely

    to lie in the _____ of the brain.

10. **True or False:** A productive way to study brain evolution is to compare the **weight and size** of different brain regions.

    A: _____

28

11. European ethology focused on the study of ___Instinctive___ behaviors.

12. To support his theory of evolution, Darwin pointed out the evolution of the ___fossils___ record through progressively more recent geological layers, the striking ___morphological___ similarities of different living species, and the major changes that can be produced in a species by ___Selective___ breeding.

13. The recessive variant of a dichotomous trait will appear in ___1___ of the second-generation offspring.

14. Chromosomes exist in the _____ of each cell.

15. The most common errors in the duplication of chromosomes are referred to as _____.

16. Copper and Zubek (1958) demonstrated that ___enriched environments___ can overcome the negative effects of disadvantaged genes.

17. **True or False: Experiential factors** account for the fact that correlations between IQ scores for monozygotic twins reared in different homes are not 1.0.

    A: _____

18. Young males of many bird species are genetically prepared to acquire the songs of their own species during the _____ phase of song acquisition.

19. Two major neural pathways are involved in birdsong in the canary: the _____ mediates the production of song while the _____ mediates the acquisition of song.

20. **True or False:** Selective breeding studies in animals and twin studies in humans have revealed **several key psychological differences** that do not have a significant genetic component.

    A: _____

**C. Short Answer Section. In no more than 5 sentences, answer each of the following questions.**

1. *"Behavior is a product of interactions between genetics, past experience, and current perceptions."* Discuss this statement within the context of Tryon's maze-bright and maze-dull rats.

2. Why is the study of brain size a poor way to study the evolution of intellect? Describe 3 important characteristics relevant to the evolution of the human brain and intelligence.

3. Compare and contrast the functional approach and the comparative approach to the study of brain-behavior relations in humans.

4. Describe the concept of a sensitive period; provide 2 examples of this concept described in Chapter 2.

5. The Minnesota Twins study was misinterpreted in four important ways. Discuss each of these misinterpretations.

**Mark your answers to the practice examination; the correct answers follow. On the basis of your performance, plan the final stages of your studying...**

Chapter 2

## Answers to Practice Examination

### A. Multiple Choice Section

1. a, b
2. b
3. a, b
4. b, d
5. a, c
6. a, b, c

7. b, c
8. c
9. b
10. a, c, d
11. a, b, d
12. b, d

### B. Modified True/False and Fill-in-the-Blank Section

1. mammary
2. dichotomous; true-breeding
3. False; heritability estimates
4. mother; mutation
5. testosterone
6. False; meiosis; mitosis
7. Chimpanzees; 99%
8. structural
9. prefrontal cortex
10. False; evolution

11. instinctive
12. fossil; structural; selective
13. about a quarter
14. nucleus
15. mutations
16. enriched environments
17. True
18. sensory
19. descending motor pathway; anterior forebrain pathway
20. False; no psychological differences

### C. Short Answer Section

1. Mention Tryon's success at breeding "maze-bright" rats; that enriched environments can ameliorate maze-running deficits in "maze-dull" rats; that successful maze running is also guided by current perceptions of the maze and the rat's internal state.

2. Mention the lack of correlation between intelligence and brain size between or within species; that the human brain has: 1) increased in size as it evolved, due in large part to 2) an increase in the cerebrum that is characterized by 3) numerous convolutions.

3. Mention the emphasis of the functional approach on evolutionary pressures; the emphasis of the comparative approach on the evolution of different species; the idea that human beings are the products of evolution and our phylogenetic ancestors.

4. Mention that this is the period during which a particular experience must occur for it to have a significant impact on development; examples include the need for early dietary restrictions in PKU babies; the need for exposure to conspecific songs for the development of song repertoire in songbirds; the impact that enriched environments have on Tryon's maze-dull rats (there are many more!).

5. Describe the focus on nature-nurture; the focus on similarities instead of differences; the lack of novelty in the findings; and the misinterpretation of what a heritability estimate means.

---

# Chapter 3

# THE ANATOMY OF THE NERVOUS SYSTEM

## I.    Jeopardy Study Items

*With reference to Chapter 3 of BIOPSYCHOLOGY, write the correct answer to each of the following questions and the correct question for each of the following answers*

1.  What defines the border between the central nervous system and the peripheral nervous system?

2.                                          A: These are called the somatic nervous system and the autonomic nervous system.

3.  What is the difference between efferent and afferent nerves?

4.  What is the main difference between the functions of the sympathetic and the parasympathetic nervous systems?

5.                                          A: These are the 12 nerves that do not project from the spinal cord.

6.  Which <u>four</u> cranial nerves are involved with vision?

7.                                          A:  These are called the dura mater, the arachnoid membrane, and the pia mater.

33

Chapter 3

8.                                        A:  This is called cerebrospinal fluid.

9.  Identify the four large internal chambers of the brain.

10.  What is choroid plexus?

11.                                       A:  This is a condition that results when the flow of CSF
                                          through the ventricles is blocked.

12.  What is the blood-brain barrier?

13.                                       A:  This is so important that it is moved across the blood-
                                          brain barrier by active transport.

14.                                       A:  These are neurons and support cells.

15.  What are neurons?

16.  List the nine major external features of a typical neuron.

17.  These determine many of the cell membrane's functional
     properties.

18.                                    A: This type of neuron has little or no axonal process.

19. What is the difference between nuclei and ganglia in the
    nervous system?

20.                                    A: This is a bundle of axons in the PNS.

21.                                    A: These are glial cells and satellite cells.

22. These glia are thought to play a role in the passage of
    chemicals from the blood into neurons.

23. Why is there normally little axonal regeneration in the
    mammalian CNS?

24. Why was the Golgi stain such a revolutionary technique
    for early neuroanatomists?

25.                                    A: This type of stain only marks structures in neuron cell
                                          bodies.

26.                                    A: This is a technique that can reveal the fine structural
                                          details of the nervous system.

27. What is the difference between anterograde and
    retrograde tract tracing?

28. What are the 3 axes for directions in the nervous
    system?

29.                                        A: This is called a midsagittal section

30. What are the names of the two ventral arms of gray
    matter visible in a cross section of the spinal cord?

31.                                        A: These are called the dorsal root ganglia.

32. Name the five major divisions of the human brain.

33. What is the other name for the midbrain?

34. Which division of the human brain undergoes the
    greatest amount of growth during development?

35.                                        A: This collection of nuclei is involved in sleep, attention,
                                           movement, maintenance of muscle tone, cardiac and
                                           respiratory reflexes

36.                                        A: These are the cerebellum and pons.

37. Identify the 2 pairs of bumps that form the mammalian
    tectum. What are their functions?

38. Where is the periaqueductal gray? What role does it
    have in mediating the effects of opiate drugs?

39.                                        A: This is called the massa intermedia.

40.                                        A: These include the lateral geniculate, medial geniculate, and ventral posterior nuclei.

41.                                        A: This is the optic chiasm.

42. What does *lissencephalic* mean?

43. What is the corpus callosum?

44. Identify the four lobes of the cerebral hemispheres.

45.                                        A: This is identified by its six layers of cells.

46. Describe three important characteristics of neocortex anatomy.

47. Name the structures that make up the limbic system.

48.                                        A: These include the globus pallidus, the putamen, the caudate, and the amygdala

49. What is the relationship between the amygdala, the limbic system, and the basal ganglia?

50. What is Parkinson's Disease, and how is related to the striatum?

---

**Once you have completed the jeopardy study items, study them. Practice bidirectional studying; make sure that you know the correct answer to every question and the correct question for every answer.**

Chapter 3

## II.    Essay Study Questions

*Using Chapter 3 of BIOPSYCHOLOGY, write an outline of the answer to each of the following essay study questions.*

1.  Describe the different kinds of cells that comprise the nervous system.

2.  Compare and contrast the function of oligodendroglia in the CNS and Schwann cells in the PNS.

3.  How do the Golgi stain, Nissl stains, myelin stains, and electron microscopy complement one another in the study the anatomy of the nervous system?

4. Compare techniques that are used for anterograde and retrograde tracing in the nervous system. When would you use each type of technique?

5. Name the structures that comprise the basal ganglia, and describe the function of this system.

6. Describe the anatomy and function of the afferent and efferent branches of the peripheral nervous system.

7. Describe the embryological development of the five major divisions of the brain.

8. What are the five major divisions of the human brain? Describe the key functions of each division.

9. Where is the reticular activating system located? Describe at least two functions of this structure.

When you have answered the essay study questions, memorize your outlines to prepare for your upcoming examination.

### III.   Practice Examination

*After completing most of your studying of Chapter 3, but at least 24 hours before your formal examination, write the following practice examination.*

**A. Multiple-Choice Section.**  Circle the correct answer for each question; *REMEMBER that some questions may have more than one correct answer.*

1. The first two cranial nerves in the mammalian brain are the:

   a.  vagus nerve.
   b.  olfactory nerve.
   c.  occulomotor nerve.
   d.  optic nerve.

2. Between the arachnoid mater and the pia mater, there:

   a.  are large blood vessels.
   b.  is the subarachnoid space.
   c.  is CSF.
   d.  are cerebral ventricles

3. The function of CSF is:

   a.  to filter the blood before it enters the brain.
   b.  to support and cushion the brain.
   c.  to ensure that the cortex does not collapse into the ventricles.
   d.  to moisten the brain.

4. Nissl stains allow researchers to see:

   a.  only a few neurons in each section.
   b.  individual neurons that are stained completely black.
   c.  myelinated axons.
   d.  neuron cell bodies.

5. Which of the following terms can refer to bundles of axons in the nervous system?

   a.  tract  — in CNS
   b.  nucleus
   c.  nerve  —  in PNS
   d.  ganglion

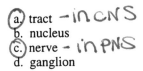

6. Which of the following anatomical planes of section could include both eyes?

   a.  a horizontal section
   b.  a coronal section
   c.  a midsaggital section.
   d.  a frontal section.

Chapter 3

7. The periaqueductal gray, the red nucleus, and the substantia nigra are all part of the:

   a. tegmentum.
   b. mesencephalon.
   c. diencephalon.
   d. telencephalon.

8. The massa intermedia and the lateral geniculate nuclei are part of the:

   a. myelencephalon.
   b. metencephalon.
   c. telencephalon.
   d. diencephalon.

9. The proteins that are embedded in the lipid bilayer of the neural membrane may include:

   a. neurotransmitters.
   b. channel proteins.
   c. signal proteins.
   d. myelin.

10. The hippocampus:

   a. is an example of neocortex.
   b. has only three cell layers.
   c. is located in the temporal lobe.
   d. is pyramidal shaped.

**B. Modified True-False and Fill-in-the Blank Section**. If the statement is true, write TRUE in the blank provided. If the statement is false, write FALSE as well as the word or words that will make the statement true if they replaced the highlighted word or words in the original statement. If the statement is incomplete, write the word or words that will complete it.

1. According to neuroanatomical arithmetic:

   a) PNS - ANS = ____Somatic____ nervous system

   b) CNS - brain = ____spinal chord____

   c) sympathetic + parasympathetic = ____autonomic____ nervous system

2. **True or False: The <u>dorsal root ganglia</u> contains the cell bodies of motor neurons.**

   A: ____FALSE  SENSORY  VENTRAL____

3. The third and fourth ventricles are connected by the ____Cerebral aquaduct____.

4. Neurons with short--or no--axonal processes are called ____internerons____.

5. The three protective membranes that enclose the brain and spinal cord are called the _____,
   the _____, and the _____.

42

6. Axonal regeneration in the PNS is possible because ___Schwann cells___ guide the regenerating axons.

7. The corpus callosum and all the other commissures would be transected by a ___midsagital___ cut through the brain.

8. The optic chiasm is the structure through which axons of some visual-system neurons ___decussate___ to the other side of the brain.

9. **True or False:** The two major structures of the metencephalon are the **thalamus and hypothalamus.**

    A: ___pons cerebellum___

10. The basal ganglia motor system includes the amygdala, the striatum, and the ___globus pallidus___

11. **True or False:** The **colliculi** are a pair of hypothalamic nuclei located on the ventral or inferior surface of the human brain, just behind the pituitary gland.

    A: ___Tectum posterior (mesencephalon)___

12. During the development of the nervous system, the telencephalon and the diencephalon are derived from the ___forebrain___.

13. **True or False:** The **parasympathetic nervous system** would be most active just after you eat a big meal.

    A: _____

14. Cerebrospinal fluid is produced by the ___choroid plexus___, and is reabsorbed from the subarachnoid space into the ___dural sinuses___.

15. **True or False:** The **central sulcus** divides the left and right hemispheres of the brain.

    A: ___longitudinal fissure___

43

## C. Diagrams

**Figure 1.** Label the 10 structures highlighted on the following drawing of the lateral surface of the human brain.

A: _____

B: _____

C: _____

D: _____

E: _____

F: _____

G: _____

H: _____

I: _____

J: _____

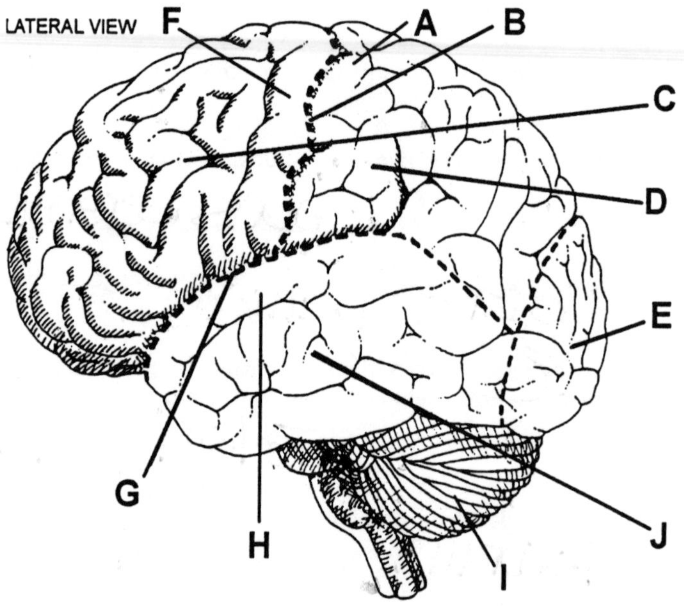

LATERAL VIEW

**Figure 2.** Label the 8 major external features of a typical neuron.

A: _____

B: _____

C: _____

D: _____

E: _____

F: _____

G: _____

H: _____

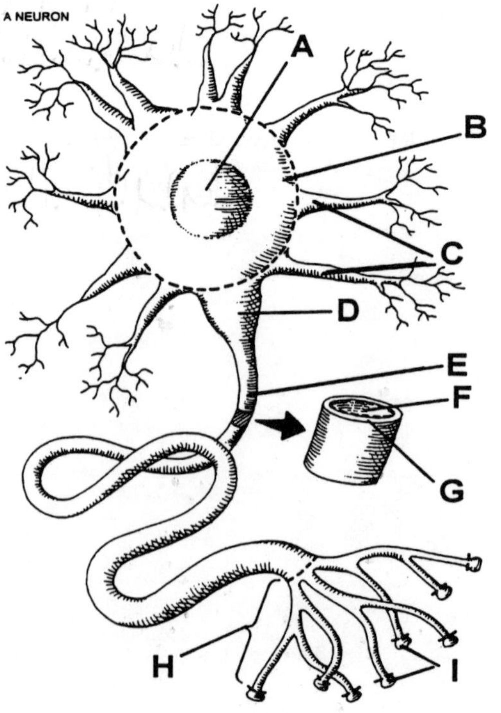

A NEURON

**D. Short Answer Section.  In no more than 5 sentences, answer each of the following questions.**

1.  Describe the functions of the major structures of the diencephalon.

2.  Describe the difference between multipolar neurons, bipolar neurons, unipolar neurons, and interneurons.

3.  Identify the two major subcortical "systems" that were described in Chapter 3.  Why is it misleading to call these collections of structures "systems"?

---

| **Mark your answers to the practice examination; the correct answers follow.  On the basis of your performance, plan the final stages of your studying.** |
| --- |

## Answers to Practice Examination

### A. Multiple Choice Section

1. b, d
2. a, b, c
3. b
4. d
5. a, c

6. a, b, d
7. a, b
8. d
9. b, c
10. b, c

### B. Modified True/False and Fill-in-the-Blank Section

1. a. somatic nervous system
   b. spinal cord
   c. autonomic nervous system
2. False; ventral horns
3. cerebral aqueduct
4. interneurons
5. dura mater; arachnoid mater; pia mater.
6. Schwann cells
7. midsagittal

8. decussate (or cross over)
9. False; pons and cerebellum
10. globus pallidus
11. False; mammillary bodies
12. Forebrain
13. True (Just remember "Rest'n'Digest!")
14. Choroid plexus; dural sinuses
15. False; longitudinal fissure

### C. Figures

**Figure 1:** A) Postcentral Gyrus  B) Central Sulcus  C) Frontal Lobe  D) Parietal Lobe  E) Occipital Lobe
F) Precentral Gyrus  G) Lateral Fissure  H) Superior Temporal Gyrus  I) Cerebellum  J) Temporal Lobe

**Figure 2:** A) Nucleus  B) Soma/Cell Body  C) Dendrites  D) Axon Hillock  E) Axon  F) Cytoplasm
G) Cell Membrane/Lipid Bilayer  H) Axonal Branches  I) Terminal Buttons

### D. Short Answer Section

1. Mention that the diencephalon has two major structures, the thalamus and hyothalamus; discuss the sensory relay function of the thalamic nuclei; discuss the role of the hypothalamus in the regulation of motivated behaviors.

2. Mention that the number of processes define each class of neuron; that mulitpolar neurons have multiple dendrites and a single axon, that bipolar neurons have a single dendrite and a single axon, that unipolar neurons have just a single process leaving the cell body, and that interneurons have a short axon or no axon at all.

3. Mention the amygdala, the caudate and putamen, and the globus pallidus of the basal ganglia; mention the amygdala (note that it is shared between these "systems"), the cingulate gyrus, the fornix, the hippocampus, the mammillary bodies, and the septum of the limbic system. Note that uncertainty about the exact anatomy and function of these systems indicates that it may be premature to view them as unitary systems.

# Chapter 4

## NEURAL CONDUCTION AND
## SYNAPTIC TRANSMISSION

## I.  Jeopardy Study Items

*With reference to Chapter 4 of BIOPSYCHOLOGY, write the correct answer to each of the following questions and the correct question for each of the following answers.*

1. What is a membrane potential, and how is it recorded?

2.                                                        A: This is usually about  -70 millivolts

3. What are the four factors that influence the distribution of
   ions on either side of a neural membrane?

4. Why is the neural membrane said to be "polarized"?

5.                                                        A:  This is called a concentration gradient.

6.                                                        A: These are sodium-potassium pumps.

7. What do EPSP's do to the membrane potential?

8. Postsynaptic potentials are said to be "graded"; what does this mean?

9. What is the difference between an EPSP and an IPSP?

10. The spread of postsynaptic potentials has two key characteristics; what are they?

11.                                         A: This is called neural integration.

12. Identify the three kinds of spatial summation.

13. Identify the two kinds of temporal summation.

14. Why is the spatial proximity of a synapse to the axon hillock so important?

15. What is responsible for reestablishing the resting potential after an action potential has occurred?

16. The absolute and relative refractory periods are responsible for two important properties of neural activity. What are they?

17.                                         A: This is the absolute refractory period.

18. What prevents action potentials from reversing direction and being conducted backwards?

19. The conduction of action potentials is active; what does this mean?

20.                                          A: This is called antidromic conduction.

21. What is a node of Ranvier?

22.                                          A: This is called saltatory conduction.

23.                                          A: In addition to myelin, this increases the speed of axonal conduction.

24. What two factors determine the speed of axonal transmission?

25. What are the four types of synapses?

26. What is the Golgi complex, and what is its function?

27. Where are peptide and nonpeptide transmitters synthesized and packaged?

28.                                          A: This process is initiated by an influx of calcium ions.

29. What is exocytosis?

30. What kind of neurotransmitter is released gradually, as Ca2+ ions accumulate in the terminal?

31. Why is it advantageous for a single neurotransmitter to have several different receptor subtypes?

32.                                          A: This is an ionotropic receptor.

33. What is a second messenger?

34.                                          A: This is an autoreceptor.

35. How is acetylcholine deactivated in the synaptic cleft?

36.                                          A: These include the amino acid neurotransmitters, the monoamine neurotransmitters, the neuropeptides, and acetylcholine.

37. What kind of neurotransmitters are glutamate, aspartate, glycine, and GABA?

38.                                    A: These include dopamine, norepinephrine, and
    epinephrine.

39. In what sequence are the catecholamines synthesized from tyrosine?

40.                                    A: The precursor for this neurotransmitter is tryptophan.

41. In what way are the gas-soluble neurotransmitters different than traditional neurotransmitters?

42.                                    A: These are neurotransmitters like the endorphins.

43. What is a neuromodulator?

44. What are agonists and antagonists?

45.                                    A: This is called a receptor blocker.

46. How does cocaine alter the function of the catecholamine neurotransmitters?

Chapter 4

47. Describe the behavioral effects of cocaine.

48. What are the behavioral effects of benzodiazepines?

49.                                          A: These increase the binding of GABA to GABA-A receptors.

50. How does atropine exert its effects?

51.                                          A: This alters neural function by blocking nicotinic acetylcholine receptors.

52.                                          A: These include muscarinic and nicotinic receptors.

---

**Once you have completed the jeopardy study items, study them. Practice bidirectional studying; make sure that you know the correct answer to every question and the correct question for every answer.**

## II. Essay Study Questions

*Using Chapter 4 of BIOPSYCHOLOGY, write an outline of the answer to each of the following essay study questions.*

1. Explain the ionic basis of the resting membrane potential

2. Briefly describe the processes of temporal summation and spatial summation of postsynaptic potentials.

3. Explain the ionic basis of the action potential.

4. Compare and contrast postsynaptic potentials and action potentials.

5. Compare and contrast the synthesis, release and inactivation of small-molecule and large-molecule neurotransmitters.

6. Discuss the functional significance of the diversity of neurotransmitters AND receptors for each neurotransmitter that is observed in the nervous system.

7. A neurotransmitter can influence a postsynaptic neuron through either ionotropic or metabotropic receptors. Compare and contrast the effect that each type of receptor has on the function of the postsynaptic neuron.

8. Describe each of the seven general steps involved in the process of synaptic transmission.

9. Compare and contrast the mechanisms of action of cocaine and the benzodiazepines.

When you have answered the essay study questions, memorize your outlines to prepare for your upcoming examination.

Chapter 4

## III.   Practice Examination

> After completing most of your studying of Chapter 4, but at least 24 hours before your formal examination, write the following practice examination.

**A. Multiple-Choice Section.**  Circle the correct answer for each question; *REMEMBER that some questions may have more than one correct answer.*

1.  In contrast to the classical neurotransmitters, neuropeptides are:

    a.  synthesized in terminal buttons.
    b.  synthesized in the cell body.
    c.  released in a pulse corresponding to the arrival of each action potential.
    d.  released gradually, reflecting a general increase in intracellular $Ca^{+2}$ ions.


2.  Which of the following is not true?

    a.  $Na^+$ ions leak continuously into resting neurons.
    b.  $K^+$ ions leak continuously out of resting neurons.
    c.  The pressure for $Na^+$ ions to move down their concentration gradient and into a resting neuron is counteracted by their electrostatic gradient.
    d.  The pressure for $K^+$ ions to move down their concentration gradient and out of a resting neuron is partially offset by their electrostatic gradient.


3.  Conduction of action potentials in *myelinated* axons is normally:

    a.  active.
    b.  passive.
    c.  orthodromic.
    d.  decremental


4.  In some neurons, the binding of a neurotransmitter to its receptors:

    a.  opens chemically-gated ion channels.
    b.  closes voltage-gated ion channels.
    c.  initiates the synthesis of second messengers.
    d.  initiates a PSP.


5.  Axoaxonic synapses are:

    a.  directed synapses.
    b.  responsible for presynaptic inhibition.
    c.  elicit IPSPs.
    d.  responsible for  receptor down-regulation.

6. In some neurons, neurotransmitter is released from a series of varicosities along the axon and its branches in additional to its terminal buttons. These varicosities are:

a. responsible for synaptic inactivation.
b. axodendritic synapses.
c. directed synapses.
d. nondirected synapses.

7. Coexistence refers to:

a. the situation in which two or more transmitters are found in the same terminal button.
b. the presence of synthetic and degradative enzymes in the same terminal button.
c. two or more presynaptic terminals forming a synapse with a single postsynaptic neuron.
d. the degradation of a large protein into two or more neurotransmitters.

8. Which of the following is an amino acid neurotransmitter?

a. GABA
b. aspartate          glycine
c. acetylcholine
d. glutamate

9. A neuron can regulate release of its own neurotransmitter through the action of:

a. a special type of metabotropic receptor.
b. axosomatic synapses
c. presynaptic autoreceptors
d. IPSPs

10. Action potentials that have been conducted half-way down the axon cannot change direction and move back towards the axon hillock and cell body because:

a. the ion channels only open in one direction.
b. the action potential depletes local extracellular Na+ ions outside of the neuron.
c. the area of the axon that has just participated in the action potential is in an absolute refractory period.
d. myelin ensures that the action potential only travels in one direction.

11. Norepinephrine is to endorphin as:

a. small-molecule neurotransmitters are to large-molecule neurotransmitters.
b. cell body synthesis is to terminal synthesis.
c. terminal synthesis is to cell body synthesis.
d. pulsed release is to gradually increasing release.

12. Neurotransmitters can be inactivated by:

a. exocytosis.
b. reuptake.
c. degradation.
d. inhibition.

**B. Modified True-False and Fill-in-the Blank Section.** If the statement is true, write TRUE in the blank provided. If the statement is false, write FALSE as well as the word or words that will make the statement true if they replaced the highlighted word or words in the original statement. If the statement is incomplete, write the word or words that will complete it.

1. **True or False:** The monoamine neurotransmitter that is not a catecholamine is **epinephrine.**

   A: _____Seritonin_____

2. A _____ is a chemical transmitter that does not itself induce signals in other cells; instead, it adjusts the sensitivity of populations of cells to the excitatory or inhibitory effects of conventional neurotransmitters.

3. **True or False:** Motor neurons release the neurotransmitter **glutamate.**

   A: _____

4. Membrane potentials are recorded between a large _____ electrode and a thinner _____ electrode.

5. A passive property and an active property of neural membranes both contribute to the uneven distribution of ions across the membrane. These are the passive _____ of the neural membrane and the active _____, respectively.

6. **True or False:** At rest, the key factor keeping the $Na^+$ ions that are outside a neuron from being driven into it by their high external concentration and the positive external charge is the **sodium/potassium pump.**

   A: _____

7. A shift in the membrane potential of a neuron from -70 to -68 mV is called a _____ de _ polarization.

8. After an action potential, the sodium-potassium pump plays only a minor role in the restoration of the

   _____.

9. The monoamine epinephrine is synthesized from its neurotransmitter precursor,

   _____dopamine_____. norepinephrine

10. During an action potential, the membrane potential is depolarized to about +50 mV by the influx of

    _____Na⁺_____ ions.

11. **True or False:** Vesicles are transported from the cell body to terminal buttons by **the action potential.**

    A: _____microtubules_____

12. **True or False:** The <u>synaptic cleft</u> protects neurotransmitters from degradation by cytoplasmic enzymes.

   A: _____

13. The _____ neurotransmitters are produced in the cell body and immediately diffuse through the cell membrane into the extracellular fluid to influence nearby cells.

14. The two forces that influence the movement and distribution of ions across the neural membrane are

   _____ and _____.

15. **True or False:** Benzodiazepines are <u>antagonists</u> at GABAergic receptors in the nervous system.

   A: _____ *agonists* _____

16. Which of the following terms describe postsynaptic potentials (PSPs), which describe action potentials (APs), and which describe both types of membrane potentials?

   a. graded _____ *PSP* _____
   b. instantaneous transmission _____ *PSD* _____
   c. integrated _____ *PSP* _____

   d. active transmission _____ *AP* _____
   e. saltatory _____ *AP* _____
   f. All-or-None _____ *AP* _____

17. An _____ *agonist* _____ is a drug that facilitates the activity of a neurotransmitter at a synapse by enhancing its release, blocking its inactivation, or mimicking the effects of the transmitter at its receptors.

18. **True or False:** <u>Postsynaptic receptors</u> refer to receptors on a neuron that are activated by the same neurotransmitter that the neuron releases.

   A: _____ *Presynaptic* _____

19. **True or False:** Myelinated conduction of the action potential is <u>faster but uses more energy</u> than nonmyelinated conduction of the action potential.

   A: _____ *FASTER MORE ENERGY EFFICIENT* _____

20. The _____ *Axon Hillock* _____ is the part of the neuron that integrates all of the excitatory and inhibitory postsynaptic potentials received by the neuron.

## C. Diagrams.

**Figure 1.** Identify the type of membrane potential (e.g., resting, EPSP/IPSP, AP, AHP) indicated by each arrow, the key type of channel (i.e., leak, chemically gated, or voltage-gated) that is open at each time point, and whether Na+ and/or K+ ions are moving into or out of the neuron,.

A. _____

B. _____

C. _____

D. _____

E. _____

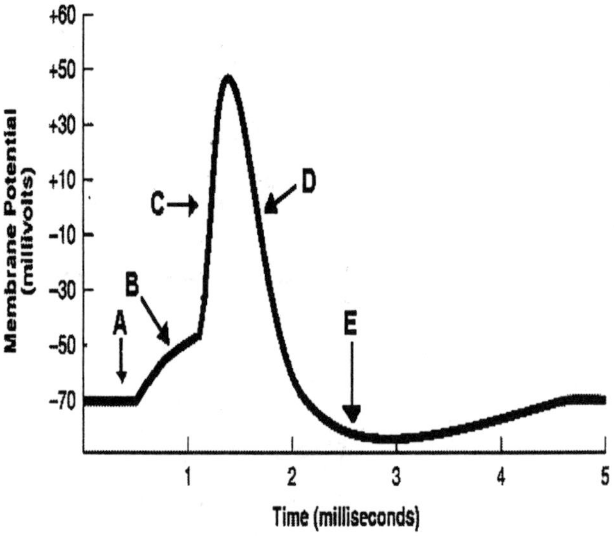

**Figure 2.** Identify the following 8 structures of a typical synapse.

A. _____

B. _____

C. _____

D. _____

E. _____

F. _____

G. _____

H. _____

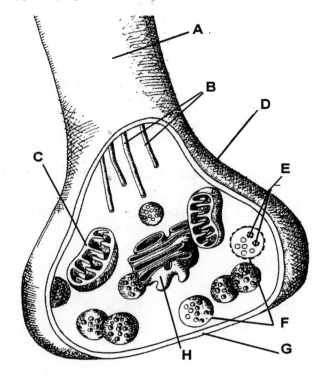

**D. Short Answer Section.  In no more than 5 sentences, answer each of the following questions.**

1.  What determines whether or not a stimulated neuron will generate an action potential?

2.  Describe the process of saltatory conduction and its advantages over the conduction action potentials in unmyelinated axons.

3.  Describe the synthesis of epinephrine, mentioning each of the intermediate neurotransmitters that are formed.

Chapter 4

4. Describe the process of exocytosis of neurotransmitter from a terminal button.

5. Describe a typical G-protein linked metabotropic receptor and the two ways that it might influence the postsynaptic neuron.

Mark your answers to the practice examination; the correct answers follow. On the basis of your performance, plan the final stages of your studying.

# Answers to Practice Examination

## A. Multiple Choice Section

| | | | |
|---|---|---|---|
| 1. b, d | 4. a, c, d | 7. a | 10. c |
| 2. c | 5. a, b | 8. a, b, d | 11. a, c, d |
| 3. a, b, c, d | 6. d | 9. a, c | 12. b, c |

## B. Modified True/False and Fill-in-the-Blank Section

1. False; serotonin
2. neuromodulator
3. False; acetylcholine
4. extracellular; intracellular
5. selective permeability; the Na+/K+ pump
6. False; impermeability of the cell membrane
7. depolarization
8. the resting membrane potential; (or ion distributions across the cell membrane)
9. norepinephrine
10. Na+
11. False; microtubules
12. False; synaptic vesicle

13. soluble gas
14. electrostatic pressure; random movement
15. False; agonists
16. a) postsynaptic potentials; action potentials
    b) postsynaptic potentials; action potentials
    c) postsynaptic potentials
    d) action potentials
    e) action potentials
    f) action potentials
17. agonist
18. False; Presynaptic autoreceptors
19. False; faster and more energy efficient
20. axon hillock

## C. Diagrams

### Figure 1.

A) resting membrane potential; leak channels; Na+ in/K+ out
B) EPSP; ligand-activated; Na+ in
C) AP depolarization; voltage-activated; Na+ in
D) AP repolarization; voltage-activated; K+ out
E) Afterhyperpolarization; voltage-activated; K+ out

**Figure 2.** A) axon B) microtubules C) mitochondria D) Terminal Button E) neurotransmitter molecules F) vesicles G) presynaptic membrane H) Golgi apparatus

## D. Short Answer Section

1. Mention the integration of postsynaptic potentials; the importance of the threshold of activation; voltage-gated channels at the axon hillock; the role of absolute and relative refractory periods.

2. Mention myelin sheaths; the importance of the nodes of Ranvier; the alternation between passive and active conduction of the action potential; the increased speed and energy efficiency of saltatory conduction.

3. Mention tyrosine; l-dopa; dopamine; norepinephrine; epinephrine.

4. Mention the action potential arriving at the terminal; the opening of voltage-activated Ca++ channels and the influx of Ca++ ions into the terminal; the synaptic vesicles fusing with the presynaptic membrane; exocytosis.

5. Mention signal proteins that cross the membrane, linking receptors outside with G-proteins inside; that G-proteins can directly elicit PSPs or act via 2nd messengers; the potential longevity of effects mediated by 2nd messengers.

<br>

# Chapter 5

## WHAT BIOPSYCHOLOGISTS DO:
## THE RESEARCH METHODS OF BIOPSYCHOLOGY

## I.    Jeopardy Study Items

*With reference to Chapter 5 of BIOPSYCHOLOGY, write the correct answer to each of the following questions and the correct question for each of the following answers.*

1. Prior to the early 1970s, what was one of the main impediments to biopsychological research?

2.                                            A: These include pneumoencephalography and cerebral angiography.

3. What is Computed Tomography?

4. What is the key advantage of the images generated by computed tomography over conventional X-rays?

5. What brain imaging technique has even greater powers of resolution than a CT scan?

6.                                            A: This technique provides information about the human brain's metabolic activity.

7. Why is radioactive 2-DG used in PET studies?

8. Describe the four advantages that functional MRI has over PET.

9. What are the five most widely studied psychophysiological measures?

10.                                     A: This is a gross measure of the electrical activity of the brain.

11. What are alpha waves?

12.                                     A: This is called a *sensory evoked potential*.

13. What is the purpose of signal averaging?

14.                                     A: These are called "far-field" potentials.

15. What does EMG stand for?

16. Why is the EMG signal usually integrated?

17. What is the main correlate of increased muscle
    contraction in an EMG signal?  What does it represent?

18.                                            A: This is measured with an electrooculogram.

19. What is the difference between skin conductance level
    and skin conductance response?

20.                                            A: This is called an ECG or EKG.

21. What does systolic blood pressure represent? What about
    diastolic blood pressure?

22.                                            A: This is called hypertension.

23. What is a sphygmomanometer?

24.                                            A: You would measure this with a plethysmograph.

25. What is stereotaxic surgery?

26.                                            A: This is called bregma.

27. Describe the 4 types of lesions used in biopsychology.

28. Although cryogenic blockade produces no brain damage, it is called a functional lesion. Why?

29. Why is it misleading to think of "the effects of an amygdala lesion"?

30.                                    A: This often elicits effects opposite that of lesions in the same area of the brain.

31. Name at least two factors that determine the effects of electrical stimulation of the brain.

32. Why are most experiments utilizing intracellular unit recording techniques done in anesthetized animals?

33.                                    A: These routes of administration include IP, IM, SC, and IV.

34. Why might it be advantageous to administer drugs intracranially?

35. What is a selective neurotoxin? Give an example of a selective neurotoxin and how you might use it to study the brain.

36. How is 2-DG used in autoradiography techniques?

37.                                    A: These techniques include *in vivo* cerebral dialysis and *in vivo* voltammetry

38.                                             A: This is called a ligand.


39. How are *in situ* hybridization and immunocytochemistry
    different?


40. What is a knockout mouse?  (No jokes about the "sweet
    science", s'il vous plait!)


41. What is a polymorphic trait?


42.                                             A: This is called a transgenic mouse.


43.                                             A: This is called a behavioral paradigm.


44. What are the three ways that neuropsychological tests
    can help brain-damaged patients?


45.                                             A: This approach to neuropsychology involves a general set
                                                of neuropsychological tests, followed by a second,
                                                customized series of tests.


46. Describe three benefits of the customized-test-battery
    approach to neuropsychological testing.


47. What is the WAIS?

48. What is the token test used for?

49. What are the sodium amytal test and the dichotic
    listening test used for?

50.                                          A:  This is called repetition priming.

51. What are the 3 fundamental problems with speech that
    brain-damaged patients might display?

52. What is the Wisconsin Card Sorting Task?  What kind of
    patient perseverates on this task?

53.                                          A:  This is called a constituent cognitive processes.

54. What are *species-common* behaviors?

55.                                          A: This is called thigmotaxis.

56. Describe the behaviors of an fearful rat in an open-field
    test.

57.                                          A:  These behaviors include piloerection, lateral approach,
                                                 and flank- and back-biting behaviors.

58. Why would you use an elevated plus maze to study a drug's effects?

59.                                          A: These behaviors include lordosis, mounts, intromissions, and ejaculations.

60. What is an unconditional stimulus in a Pavlovian conditioning paradigm.

61. What is the difference between Pavlovian and operant conditioning?

62. Research on conditioned taste aversion challenged three widely held principles of learning; what were they?

63.                                          A: It is assessed with a radial arm maze or the Morris Maze.

64. What is conditioned defensive burying?

65. What is meant by the term "converging operations"?

---

**Once you have completed the jeopardy study items, study them. Practice bidirectional studying; make sure that you know the correct answer to every question and the correct question for every answer.**

## II.     Essay Study Questions

*Using Chapter 5 of BIOPSYCHOLOGY, write an outline of the answer to each of the following essay study questions.*

1. Compare and contrast MRI and PET imaging techniques.

2. Explain why and how evoked potentials are averaged.

3. Compare the following kinds of electrophysiological recording:  EEG recording, intracellular unit recording, extracellular unit recording, and multiple-unit recording.

4. Compare the different methods for producing brain lesions; include cyrogenic blockade and selective neurotoxins. Describe 2 situations when you might prefer one method over another.

5. Describe four of the tests that a neuropsychologist would use to assess the emotional, motivational, or intellectual function of a patient suspected of suffering from impaired neural function.

6. Describe two reasons why the behavioral effects of aspiration/electrolytic/radio-frequency/cryogenic brain lesions can be difficult to interpret. Describe two techniques you might use to reduce these problems.

7. What impact did the discovery of conditioned taste aversions have on theories of animal learning and the ways in which biopsychologists study animal learning in the laboratory?

8. Using any combination of the methods that you learned about in Chapter 5 of BIOPSYCHOLOGY, design an experiment that would reveal the function of prefrontal cortex.

9. Compare and contrast gene knockout techniques and gene replacement techniques in the study of brain-behavior relations. Describe some of the caveats one must keep in mind when examining research that uses these techniques.

---

**When you have answered the essay study questions, memorize your outlines to prepare for your upcoming examination.**

Chapter 5

## III. Practice Examination

> *After completing most of your studying of Chapter 5, but at least 24 hours before your formal examination, write the following practice examination.*

**A. Multiple-Choice Section.** Circle the correct answer for each question; *REMEMBER that some questions may have more than one correct answer.*

1. Which of the following is a contrast X-ray technique that is used for studying the brain?

   a. angiography
   b. MRI
   c. pneumoencephalography
   d. PET

2. Which of the following is a measure of the background level of skin conductance associated with a particular situation?

   a. SCR
   b. SCL
   c. P300
   d. ECG

3. Functional MRI has several advantages over PET imaging of the brain. These include:

   a. it is faster.
   b. it provides both structural and functional information.
   c. it has better spatial resolution.
   d. it can be done in awake, behaving subjects.

4. Which of the following can be determined by extracellular unit recording?

   a. the amplitude of EPSPs and IPSPs
   b. the amplitude of APs
   c. temporal summation
   d. the rate of firing

5. The size and shape of a radio-frequency lesion is determined by:

   a. the duration and intensity of the current.
   b. the size of the subject.
   c. the configuration of the electrode
   d. the location of the electrode.

6. Which of the following can be used to destroy neurons whose cell bodies are in an area without destroying neurons whose axons are merely passing through?

   a. ibotenic acid
   b. 6-hydroxydopamine
   c. kainic acid
   d. aspiration

7. Invasive techniques used to study brain-behavior relations include:

    a. plethysmography
    b. extracellular single unit recording
    c. *in vivo* microdialysis
    d. functional MRI

8. Spatial memory in rats is often studied using:

    a. a conditioned defensive burying paradigm.
    b. a Morris water maze.
    c. a conditioned taste aversion.
    d. a radial-arm maze.

9. The major objectives of behavioral research methods are to:

    a. produce the behavior under study and then objectively measure it.
    b. control, simplify, and objectify behavior.
    c. study behavior performed by subjects in their natural environment.
    d. eliminate behavioral problems in subjects.

10. The paired-image subtraction technique involves:

    a. obtaining CT images from several different subjects.
    b. subtracting PET or fMRI images generated during one task from images generated during another.
    c. examining differences between far-field potentials.
    d. combining differences in electrical activity recorded between the front and back of the eye.

**B. Modified True-False and Fill-in-the Blank Section.** If the statement is true, write TRUE in the blank provided. If the statement is false, write FALSE as well as the word or words that will make the statement true if they replaced the highlighted word or words in the original statement. If the statement is incomplete, write the word or words that will complete it.

1. **True or False:** **Cerebral angiography** has higher powers of resolution than CT.

    A: _MRI_

2. Unlike CT and traditional MRI imaging techniques, __PET; FMRI__ scans provide information about the metabolic activity of the brain.

3. What do the following abbreviations stand for?
    a. PET: _Position Emission Tomography_
    b. MRI: _Magnetic Resonance Imaging_
    c. CT: _Computed tomography_

4. In humans, EEG electrodes are usually placed on the _Scalp_.

5. In EEG recordings, alpha waves are associated with _relaxation awake_.

Chapter 5

6. True or False: In **bipolar EEG recording**, one electrode is attached on the target site and the other is attached to a point of relative electrical silence such as the ear lobe.

A: _____MONOPOLAR_____

7. True or False: The electrophysiological technique for recording eye movements is called **electromyography**.

A: _____Electro oculography_____

8. _____steriotaxic_____ surgery involves the placement of an electrode or some other device at a specific target site in the brain.

9. Reversible lesions of neural tissue can be accomplished using _____cryogenic_____ blockade or by injecting _____local anesthetics_____ directly into the brain.

10. The sodium amytal test is a test of language _____lateralization_____.

11. True or False: **Extracellular single-unit recording techniques** allow a researcher to record the electrical activity of single neurons in a freely-moving animal.

A: _____

12. The location of a particular neurotransmitter in the brain can be determined using techniques such as _____ or _____.

13. A set of procedures developed for the investigation of a particular behavioral phenomenon is commonly referred to as a _____.

14. _____ techniques may allow researchers to turn genes off and on at will.

15. Patients with frontal-lobe lesions often display _____ the Wisconsin Card Sorting Test.

16. Behaviors that are displayed by virtually all members of a species that are the same age and sex are called _____ behaviors.

17. What might each of the following behavioral paradigms be used to study?

    a. open field: _____

    b. self-administration box: _____

    c. radial-arm maze: _____

    d. Morris water maze: _____

---

# Chapter 6

# HUMAN BRAIN DAMAGE AND ANIMAL MODELS

---

## I.    Jeopardy Study Items

*With reference to Chapter 6 of BIOPSYCHOLOGY, write the correct answer to each of the following questions and the correct question for each of the following answers.*

1.  What are meningiomas?

2.                                              A:  This is called an encapsulated tumor.

3.  What is the difference between a benign tumor and a
     malignant tumor?

4.                                              A:  This is called an infiltrating tumor.

5.  What is a metastatic tumor; where do most metastatic
     brain tumors come from?

6.  What is a tumor suppressor gene?

7.                                              A:  This is called a stroke.

8. What is an aneurysm?

9.                                        A: These include thrombosis, embolism, and arteriosclerosis.

10. What is the difference between a thrombus and an embolus?

11. Which neurotransmitter is thought to play a key role in stroke-related brain damage?

12. List three key properties of ischemia-induced brain damage.

13.                                        A: This is called a hematoma.

14.     What is a contre-coup injury?

15. What is the difference between a contusion and a concussion?

16.                                        A: This is called punch-drunk syndrome.

17.    What is encephalitis?

18.   This condition results when a bacterial infection attacks
       and inflames the meninges.

19.                                          A: This is called general paresis; it may result from a
                                             syphilitic infection.

20.   What is the difference between a neurotropic and a
      pantropic viral infection?

21.                                          A:  These include the mumps and herpes viruses.

22.   What is a toxic psychosis?  Give one example of a toxic
      psychosis.

23.                                          A:  This was caused by the mercury used to make felt hats in
                                             the 18th century.

24.   What is tardive dyskinesia?

25.   What is the difference between exogenous and
      endogenous neurotoxins?

26.                                          A: This is called multiple sclerosis.

27. Which genetic abnormality is associated with Down's syndrome?

28. What are the symptoms of Down's syndrome?

29. Why are genetic abnormalities rarely associated with dominant genes?

30. What is unusual about the gene that underlies the development of Huntington's disease?

31.                                                   A: This is called apoptosis.

32. What is the difference between apoptosis and necrosis.

33.                                                   A: This is called epilepsy.

34. What is the difference between a seizure and a convulsion?

35. What is an epileptic aura? Why are they important in the diagnosis and management of epilepsy?

36.                                                    A: These include either generalized or partial seizures.

37. Why is epilepsy considered to be a number of different,
    though related, diseases?

38. What is the difference between a simple partial seizure
    and a complex partial seizure?

39.                                                    A: This is called a psychomotor attack.

40. What are the differences between grand mal and petit
    mal seizures?

41. Describe the symptoms of a grand mal seizure.

42.                                                    A: This is called a *petit mal absence* seizure

43. What are the major symptoms of Parkinson's disease?

44.                                                    A:  This is l-dopa.

45. What helps to initiate the synthesis of dopamine?  Why
    is this potentially significant in the treatment of
    Parkinson's disease?

46. What is the genetic basis of Huntington's disease?


47. What are the symptoms of Huntington's disease?


48.                                          A: This is called Huntingtin.


49. Describe the neuropathology that underlies multiple
      sclerosis.


50. What are the symptoms of multiple sclerosis?


51.                                          A: This is the study of various factors that influence the
                                             distribution of disease in the general population.


52. What is experimental allergic encephalomyelitis?


53. What are the symptoms of Alzheimer's disease?


54.                                          A: neurofibrillary tangles and amyloid plaques


55.                                          A: These areas include the entorhinal cortex, hippocampus,
                                             and amygdala.


56. What evidence suggests that Alzheimer's disease is not
      due to a single genetic factor?

57. What kind of over-the-counter medication may be helpful in the treatment of Alzheimer's disease?

58.                                    A: This is called a homologous animal model.

59. What is the difference between a homologous animal model and an isomorphic animal model?

60.                                    A: This is called a predictive animal model

61. What is kindling?

62.                                    A: These characteristics include the fact that the underlying neural changes are permanent, and massed stimulations will not produce it

63. In what two ways does kindling model epilepsy?

64. How can a syndrome of spontaneous kindled convulsions induced?

65.                                    A: This refers to animals in which the genes of another species have been introduced.

66. List three pieces of evidence that suggest that the transgenic mouse model of Alzheimer's will be useful in the study of Alzheimer's disease.

67.                                                    A: This is the preeminent animal model of Parkinson's
                                                       disease.

68.                                                    A: This is called MPTP.

69.  What is deprenyl?  Why might it be effective in the
     treatment of Parkinson's disease?

70.                                                    A: This is called monoamine oxidase.

---

**Once you have completed the jeopardy study items, study them.  Practice bidirectional studying; make sure
that you know the correct answer to every question and the correct question for every answer.**

## II.    Essay Study Questions

*Using Chapter 6 of BIOPSYCHOLOGY, write an outline of the answer to each of the following essay
study questions.*

1. Describe the role of glutamate in the development of stroke-induced brain damage.

2. Describe the transgenic mouse model of Alzheimer's disease. Why is it such an exciting breakthrough in the study of this disease?

3. What is epilepsy? Describe the characteristics of the 2 major categories of epilepsy.

4. Parkinson's disease, Huntington's disease, and multiple sclerosis are movement disorders; compare and contrast these diseases.

5.  Describe the behavioral and neuropathological symptoms of Alzheimer's disease. What evidence suggests that it has a genetic basis?

6.  Compare homologous, isomorphic, and predictive animal models and their role in biopsychological research.

7.  Describe and discuss the kindling model of epilepsy.

When you have answered the essay study questions, memorize your outlines to prepare for your upcoming examination.

## III.  Practice Examination

*After completing most of your studying of Chapter 6, but at least 24 hours before your formal examination, write the following practice examination.*

**A. Multiple-Choice Section.**  Circle the correct answer for each question; *REMEMBER that some questions may have more than one correct answer.*

1.  Meningiomas:

   a.  grow between the meninges of the nervous system.
   b.  are usually benign tumors.
   c.  are usually metastatic tumors.
   d.  are encapsulated tumors.

2.  Infiltrating tumors are usually:

   a.  meningiomas.
   b.  benign.
   c.  malignant.
   d.  the type found in the brain

3.  Which neuropsychological disorders have a strong genetic component?

   a.  Huntington's disease
   b.  Parkinson's disease
   c.  Alzheimer's disease
   d.  epilepsy

4.  General paresis is:

   a.  an officer in the Spanish army.
   b.  caused by a viral infection.
   c.  caused by a bacterial infection.
   d.  caused by the syphilis bacteria.

5.  The mumps and herpes viruses are:

   a.  pantropic infections.
   b.  neurotropic infections.
   c.  bacterial infections.
   d.  never found in the brain.

6.  Tardive dyskinesia is produced by:

   a.  meningitis.
   b.  antipsychotic drugs.
   c.  bacterial infection.
   d.  syphilis.

7. Alzheimer's disease is characterized by the development of neurofibrillary tangles and amyloid plaques in:

   a. the occipital lobe
   b. the hippocampus
   c. inferotemporal cortex
   d. prefrontal cortex

8. Kindled convulsions have been produced:

   a. in primates.
   b. by drugs.
   c. by amygdala stimulation.
   d. by hippocampus stimulation.

9. The development of multiple sclerosis is influenced by:

   a. depletion of the neurotransmitter dopamine.
   b. environmental factors, as people raised in cool climates are more likely to develop the disease.
   c. environmental factors, as people raised in warm climates are more likely to develop the disease.
   d. genetic factors.

10. Which of the following drugs are identified neurotoxins?

    a) lead
    b) mercury
    c) MPTP
    d) alcohol

**B. Modified True-False and Fill-in-the Blank Section.** If the statement is true, write TRUE in the blank provided. If the statement is false, write FALSE as well as the word or words that will make the statement true if they replaced the highlighted word or words in the original statement. If the statement is incomplete, write the word or words that will complete it.

1. The effects of many minor concussions can accumulate to produce a serious disorder called the

   _____ syndrome.

2. **True or False: Embolism** in blood vessel walls are a common cause of intracerebral hemorrhage.

       A: _____

3. The first recorded case of _____ was reported in the town of Bures, England in 1630.

4. A _____ animal is one whose cells contain genetic material from another species..

5. A contusion is a closed head injury that results in a _____, or bruise, which often accumulates in the subdural space.

6. A parkinsonian syndrome can be induced in humans and other primates with injections of ___MPTP___.

7. **True or False:** Kindling is most rapidly produced by **massed stimulations** of the amygdala or hippocampus.

A: _____ spaced stimulations _____

8. Fill in each of the following blanks with the name of the related neurological disorder: epilepsy, Parkinson's disease, Huntington's disease, multiple sclerosis, or Alzheimer's disease.

   a. neurofibrillary tangles: _Alzheimers_

   b. chromosome 21: _Alzheimers_

   c. experimental allergic encephalomyelitis: _MS_

   d. auras: _Epilepsy_

   e. nigrostriatal pathway: _Parkinsons_

   f. psychomotor attack: _Epilepsy_

   g. choreiform movement: _Huntingtons_

   h. autoimmune disease: _MS_

9. **True or False:** The observation of **a grand mal seizure** is incontrovertible evidence of epilepsy.

A: _____

10. Much of the brain damage associated with stroke is a consequence of the excessive release of the neurotransmitter _____.

11. _____ is a motor disorder that is caused by long-term administration of some antipsychotic drugs.

12. **True or False:** Animal models that resemble human disorders but artificially produced in the lab are called **homologous models.** _isomorphic models_

A: _____

13. A particular exciting aspect to the recent work on the transgenic model of Alzheimer's disease is the fact that the infected mice show deficits in _memory_.

14. An _psychomotor attack_ is a compulsive, repetitive, simple behavior that may be displayed in some forms of epilepsy.

15. A _____ is a mass of cells that grow independently of the rest of the body.

**C. Short Answer Section. In no more than 5 sentences, answer each of the following questions.**

1. Why have recently developed genetic tests placed the offspring of parents who develop Huntington's disease in a difficult situation?

2. Describe the symptoms and neuropathology of Parkinson's disease. Describe the isomorphic model that has rejuvenated study of the disease in animal models.

3. Compare and contrast the different kinds of cerebrovascular disorders.

---

| Mark your answers to the practice examination; the correct answers follow. On the basis of your performance, plan the final stages of your studying. |
|---|

7.  Why do some animals have their eyes mounted side-by-side on the front of their heads?

8.  How does the location of our eyes--and the resulting binocular disparity--provide a basis for seeing in three dimensions?

9.                                      A:  These cells include photoreceptors, horizontal cells, bipolar cells, amacrine cells, and retinal ganglion cells.

10. Why is the circuitry of the cells in the retina backwards?

11.                                     A:  This  is called a blind spot.

12.                                     A:  This is called the fovea.

13. What is visual completion?

14.                                     A:  These are perceived by a process called surface interpolation.

15.                                     A:  These are the photoreceptors for photopic vision

16. What is scotopic vision?

17. How are rods and cones distributed over the retina?

18.                                              A: There are more of this type of photoreceptor in your nasal
                                                    hemiretinas.


19.                                              A: This is called a spectral sensitivity curve.


20. What is the Purkinje effect, and why does it occur?


21.                                              A: These are called saccades.


22. After a few moments, a simple image stabilized on the
    retina disappears. Why does this happen?


23. What does research on the perception of stabilized
    retinal images suggest about the function of eye
    movements?


24.                                              A: This process is called transduction.


25. What is a pigment?


26.                                              A: This is the photopigment found in rods.


27. What happens to rhodopsin when it is bleached?


28. How does light affect the membrane potential of rods?

29. How does light alter the release of glutamate by rods?

30. What is the retina-geniculate-striate pathway?

31.                                              A: Signals from this visual field all converge in the right primary visual cortex.

32. What does retinotopic organization refer to?

33. What is the functional significance of the optic chiasm?

34.                                              A: This pathway conveys visual information about color, fine pattern details, and slow or stationary object.

35.                                              A: This pathway conveys information about moving stimuli.

36. Why are edges such important visual stimuli?

37.                                              A: These are called Mach bands.

38. What is contrast enhancement?  What type of neural circuitry can produce contrast enhancement?

39. What is a receptive field?

40. List the four general rules that describe the receptive
    fields of retinal ganglion, lateral geniculate, and lower
    layer IV neurons in the visual system.

41.                                    A: This means that cells respond to input from just one eye.

42. What does "on firing" and "off firing" visual neurons
    mean?

43.                                    A: These are called "on-center" visual cells.

44. What happens to spike activity if you dimly illuminated
    the entire receptive field for an "off-center" visual
    neuron?

45.                                    A: These are either "simple cells" or "complex cells".

46. What are the main features of the receptive fields of
    simple cortical cells?

47. What are the main features of the receptive fields of
    complex cortical cells?

48.                                    A: These cells are likely to play a role in depth perception.

49. What accounts for the characteristics of the receptive
    fields of the cells in visual cortex?

50. Describe the flow of visual information from the lateral geniculate neurons of the thalamus to the complex cells of primary visual cortex.

51. Why is the organization of receptive field location in visual cortex said to be *columnar?*

52. What is an aggregate field?

53. What experimental results suggest that the input into lower layer IV from each eye occurs in alternating stripes?

54.                                          A: This is called a sine-wave grating.

55. What are the two key principles that underlie the spatial-frequency theory of visual cortex function?

56. What produces our perception of the achromatic colors?

57. What determines our perception of an object's color?

58.                                          A: This is called the component theory of color vision.

59. What is the opponent theory of color vision?

60.                                          A: These are called complementary colors.

61. How is a complementary afterimage formed?

62.                                          A: This technique is called microspectrophotometry.

63. What evidence suggests that there are three different kinds of cones?

64. What evidence suggests that visual system neurons respond to different wavelengths according to opponent principles?

65. What is the major advantage of color constancy in the visual system?

66. Describe Land's retinex theory of color vision.

67.                                          A: These are called dual-opponent color cells.

68.                                          A: These areas are referred to as "blobs".

Once you have completed the jeopardy study items, study them. Practice bidirectional studying; make sure that you know the correct answer to every question and the correct question for every answer.

## II.  Essay Study Questions

*Using Chapter 7 of BIOPSYCHOLOGY, write an outline of the answer to each of the following essay study questions.*

1. Describe the anatomical and functional characteristics of the P- and M-channels of the retina-geniculate-striate system.

2. How did Land (1977) demonstrate color constancy to support his retinex theory of color vision?

3. What is the duplexity theory of vision?  Describe the evidence that supports it.

4. What are spectral sensitivity curves? Draw them for the photopic and scotopic visual systems; use these figures to help explain the Purkinje effect.

5. Describe the importance of eye movements to the proper function of the visual system; include the effects of paralyzing eye movement on visual perception.

6. How is visual information from the right visual field transferred from the retinas to the primary visual cortex? In your answer, include a discussion of the retinotopic organization of the visual system.

7. Explain how lateral inhibition results in contrast enhancement and the perception of the Mach Band illusion.

8. Compare and contrast the receptive fields of complex cells, simple cells, and the neurons in lower layer IV of visual cortex.

9. Describe Hubel and Wiesel's model of visual cortex organization and the experimental results on which this model is based.

**When you have answered the essay study questions, memorize your outlines to prepare for your upcoming examination.**

Chapter 7

## III.  Practice Examination

> *After completing most of your studying of Chapter 7, but at least 24 hours before your formal examination, write the following practice examination.*

**A. Multiple-Choice Section.** Circle the correct answer for each question; *REMEMBER that some questions may have more than one correct answer.*

1.  Humans can see electromagnetic waves of energy that have a length of:

    a.  40 nanometers.
    b.  380 to 760 nanometers.
    c.  1,000 to 4,000 nanometers.
    d.  260 to 380 nanometers.

2.  The psychological correlates of wavelength and intensity are:

    a.  color and brightness, respectively.
    b.  brightness and hue, respectively.
    c.  shape and color, respectively.
    d.  brightness and shape, respectively.

3.  The adjustment of pupil size in response to changes in illumination represents a compromise between:

    a.  size and position.
    b.  color and intensity.
    c.  sensitivity and acuity.
    d.  color and shape.

4.  When rods are exposed to light, they:

    a.  become depolarized.
    b.  become hyperpolarized.
    c.  increase their release of glutamate.
    d.  decrease their release of glutamate .

5.  The photopic visual system is characterized by:

    a.  a high degree of convergence onto bipolar cells.
    b.  maximal sensitivity to light in the range of 560 nanometers.
    c.  high visual acuity.
    d.  high sensitivity.

6.  Off-center cells in the visual system could include:

    a.  rods and cones.
    b.  retinal ganglion cells.
    c.  simple cortical cells.
    d.  complex cortical cells.

7. Hubel and Wiesel injected a radioactive amino acid into one eye of their subjects, and then later they looked at the pattern of radioactivity that had been passed by anterograde transport to primary visual cortex. They observed:

   a. alternating patches of radioactivity and nonradioactivity in all cortical layers.
   b. radioactivity in only one hemisphere.
   c. alternating patches of radioactivity and nonradioactivity in lower layer IV in both hemispheres.
   d. orientation specificity.

8. The spatial-frequency theory of visual cortex function is based on the principle that any:

   a. visual array can be represented by plotting the intensity of light along lines running through it.
   b. curve can be broken down into constituent sine waves by Fourier analysis.
   c. sine-wave grating is orientation free.
   d. visual cell is more sensitive to a simple bar of light than a sine-wave grating.

9. Because of the phenomenon of color constancy, the color of an object relative to its surroundings:

   a. varies with changes in illumination.
   b. does not vary, even though there may be major changes in the wavelengths of light that it reflects.
   c. will vary depending on whether the photopic or the scotopic visual system is active.
   d. does not vary, regardless of whether the photopic or the scotopic visual system is active.

10. The retinal ganglion cells:

   a. are responsible for scotopic vision.
   b. release the excitatory neurotransmitter glutamate.
   c. transduce light energy in the range of 560 nanometers.
   d. are the most superficial layer of cells in the retina.

11. The retina-geniculate-striate system:

   a. contains neurons that are monocular.
   b. is retinotopically organized.
   c. includes ommitidia and the lateral plexus.
   d. conveys information from each eye to primary visual cortex in both hemispheres.

12. Cones are to rods as:

   a. color vision is to viewing shades of gray.
   b. photopic vision is to scotopic vision.
   c. high sensitivity is to high acuity.
   d. high convergence is to low convergence.

13. The M pathway for visual information is:

   a. responsible for conveying information about slowly moving objects.
   b. comprised of magnocellular neurons in the lateral geniculate and the retinal ganglion cells that project on them.
   c. largely responsible from conveying information from rod receptors.
   d. found in the upper four layers of the lateral geniculate nucleus of the thalamus.

**B. Modified True-False and Fill-in-the Blank Section.** If the statement is true, write TRUE in the blank provided. If the statement is false, write FALSE as well as the word or words that will make the statement true if they replaced the highlighted word or words in the original statement. If the statement is incomplete, write the word or words that will complete it.

1. **True or False:** Retinal ganglion cell axons from the **temporal hemiretinas** decussate to synapse in the lateral geniculate nucleus of the thalamus in the contralateral hemisphere.

      **A:** _____

2. Signals from an object viewed in the left visual field are projected to striate cortex in the _____ hemisphere.

3. The accentuation of differences in brightness that is perceived when adjacent areas of a stimulus vary in their intensity is called _____ enhancement; this phenomenon is evident in the _____ band illusion.

4. The "preferred" type of stimulus for most neurons of the striate cortex is a _____.

5. The _____ visual system is characterized by its high sensitivity to light, a high degree of convergence, and its poor acuity.

6. In monkeys, over half of all complex cortical cells are _____; that is, they respond best to stimulation of either eye.

7. **True or False:** The area of the visual field that is covered by the receptive fields of all of the cells in a particular column of striate cortex is called the **receptive field** of that column.

      **A:** _____

8. Microspectrophotometry experiments have confirmed the prediction of the _____ theory of color vision.

9. **True or False:** When an ommitidia receptor fires, it inhibits the activity of its neighbors because of the inhibitory interconnections of **bipolar cells.**

      **A:** _____

10. Dual-opponent color cells are distributed in striate cortex in peg-like columns that are commonly known as _____.

11. **True or False:** The M-pathway for visual information is most sensitive to **slowly moving** stimuli

      **A:** _____

12. The _____ of a photon into a neural signal occurs in the photoreceptors of the retina.

13. In the absence of _____, after a few seconds of viewing a simple stimulus disappears, leaving a featureless gray field.

14. According to the Nobel-Prize winning research of Hubel and Wiesel, primary visual cortex neurons are grouped in functional _____.

15. **True or False**: Virtually all simple cells in striate cortex are **monocular.**

   A: _____

16. According to the _____ theory of color vision, the color of a particular stimulus is encoded by the ratio of three different kinds of color receptors.

17. **True or False:** The high acuity of cone receptors in the retina is due to their **high degree of convergence** onto retinal ganglion cells.

   A: _____

18. When radioactive 2-DG is injected into a monkey that is then shown a pattern of alternating vertical stripes that are moving back and forth, alternating patches of radioactivity are produced in the _____, reflecting the orientation specificity of the cells in different functional columns.

19. **True or False:** The **P pathway** conveys information about color, fine details, and slowly moving objects through the retina-geniculate-striate pathway.

   A: _____

20. Severing the optic chiasm along the midsagittal plane would produce blindness in the visual fields for the _____ hemiretinas of each eye.

21. The perception of an edge is really the perception of a _____ between two adjacent areas of the visual field.

22. The visual system uses information provided by receptors around your blind spot to fill in the gaps in your retinal image; this phenomenon is called _____.

23. **True or False:** At night, the Purkinje effect is evident because yellow flowers appear as a **brighter shade** of gray than blue flowers.

   A: _____

24. A graph of the relative brightness of lights of the same intensity presented at different wavelengths is called a _____.

## C. Diagrams

1. Label the six different types of cells that are presented in the following diagram of the mammalian retina.

A. _____

B. _____

C. _____

D. _____

E. _____

F. _____

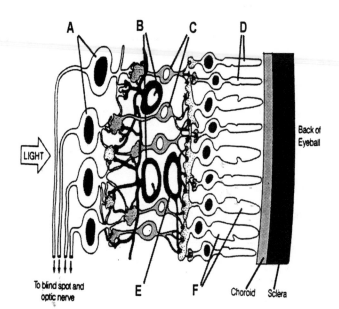

2. Label the 8 parts of the retina-geniculate-striate visual pathway indicated in the figure below.

A. _____

B. _____

C. _____

D. _____

E. _____

F. _____

G. _____

H. _____

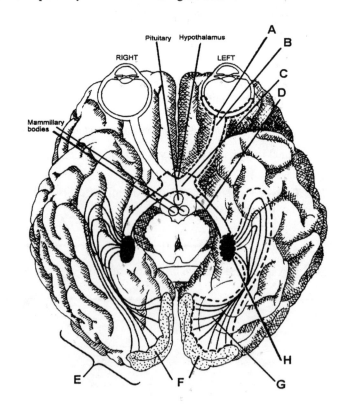

**D. Short Answer Section. In no more than 5 sentences, answer each of the following questions.**

1. Describe the spatial-frequency theory of vision.

2. "The visual system is a system of two's." Come up with at least 4 reasons why this statement is accurate.

3. What is color constancy? In what respect does color constancy create a problem for the component and opponent theories?

Mark your answers to the practice examination; the correct answers follow. On the basis of your performance, plan the final stages of your studying.

## Answers to Practice Examination

### A. Multiple Choice Section

| | |
|---|---|
| 1. b, d | 8. a, b |
| 2. a | 9. b |
| 3. c | 10. b, d |
| 4. b, d | 11. a, b, d |
| 5. b, c | 12. a, b |
| 6. a, b, c | 13. b, c |
| 7. c | |

### B. Modified True/False and Fill-in-the-Blank Section

1. False; nasal hemiretina
2. contralateral (right)
3. contrast; Mach band
4. bar of light
5. scotopic
6. binocular
7. False; aggregate field
8. component process
9. False; the lateral plexus
10. blobs
11. False; rapidly moving
12. transduction
13. saccades (movement)
14. columns
15. True
16. component-process
17. False; low degree of convergence
18. primary visual cortex
19. True
20. nasal
21. contrast
22. completion
23. False; darker
24. spectral sensitivity curve

### C. Diagrams

Figure 1. A) Retinal Ganglion Cells  B) Amacrine Cells  C) Bipolar Cells  D) Rods
E) Horizontal Cells  F) Cones

Figure 2. A) Retina (Blind Spot)  B) Optic Nerve  C) Optic Chiasm  D) Optic Tract  E) Occipital Lobe
F) Primary Visual Cortex  G) Optic Radiations  H) Lateral Geniculate Nucleus
G)

### D. Short Answer Section

1. Mention the 2 key physical principles: 1) any stimuli can be represented by a plot of the light intensity along lines running through the stimulus; and 2) any curve can be broken down into constituent sine waves by Fourier analysis; mention the idea that each functional module of visual cortex responds selectively to specific frequencies and orientations of sine-wave gratings, which are integrated into the perception of a scene; mention demonstrations that neurons in visual cortex respond better to sine wave gratings than to static bars of light.

2. Mention some combination of the following: there are 2 eyes; there are 2 types of photoreceptors; there are 2 optic nerves/tracts, 2 lateral geniculate, and 2 hemispheres of primary visual cortex; there are 2 visual systems (scotopic and photopic) and 2 visual pathways (M- and P-pathways); there are 2 types of striate cortex neurons.

3. Mention the fact that color perception is constant even when different wavelengths of light are reflected; that color perception is a function of comparing the wavelengths reflected by a stimulus with wavelengths reflected in adjacent areas in the visual field; that this cannot be accounted for by component process and opponent process theories, which suggest that perception is a strict function of the wavelength of reflected light.

## Chapter 8

## MECHANISMS OF PERCEPTION, CONSCIOUS AWARENESS, and ATTENTION

### I. Jeopardy Study Items

*With reference to Chapter 8 of BIOPSYCHOLOGY, write the correct answer to each of the following questions and the correct question for each of the following answers.*

1. exteroceptive sensory systems    A: These include vision, touch, hearing, olfaction, and taste.

2. What is the difference between primary and secondary sensory cortex? Between sensory cortex and association cortex? Association recieves input from more than one sensory system. primary recieves most of its input directly from the thalamic relay nuclei of that system, secondary recieves most of its input from the primary sensory cortex of that system

3. What is a hierarchical system? a system whose members can be assigned to specific levels or ranks in relation to one another.

4. Why are sensory systems said to have a hierarchical organization? as one moves through a sensory system receptors > thalamic nuclei > primary sensory cortex > secondary sensory cortex > association cortex neurons respond to greater and greater levels of specifity

5. Describe the general pattern of deficits that emerges from damage to progressively higher levels of any sensory system. The higher the level of damage the more specific and complex the deficit.

6. Sensation    A: This is the process of detecting the presence of a stimuli.

7. What is the difference between sensation and perception? Sensation is detecting the presence of a stimuli, whereas perception is the process of interpreting the stimuli.

111

8. organization into different areas each of which perform a different function   A: This is called functional segregation.

9. simultonius analysis of a signal in different ways by the multiple parallel pathways of a neural network.   A: This is called parallel processing.

10. What is the difference between serial processing and parallel processing?   serial processes information flows along just one pathway, parallel pathways processes information in multiple parallel pathways

11. how does the brain combine individual sensory attributes to produce integrated perception   A: This is called the *binding problem*.

12. ventral stream   A: These include the prestriate cortex and inferotemporal cortex.

13. An area of blindness in the visual field   A: This is called a scotoma.

14. When would you give someone a perimetry test?   If you suspected a scotoma

15. What is a hemianopsia?   Pt's with a scotoma covering half of their visual field

16. ability of individuals to respond to visual stimuli in their scotomas even though they have no conscious awareness of it   A: This is called blind-sight.

17. Percieved visual contours that do not exist   A: These are called subjective contours.

18. What is a visual agnosia?   a specific agnosia for visual stimuli. individuals can see the object but does not know what it is.

Mr P.

112

19. How many different functional areas are there in the visual cortices of humans? How do we know?

20. _ventral stream_

A: This visual pathway includes the ventral prestriate area and adjacent portions of inferotemporal cortex.

21. What evidence suggests that the perceptual deficits of prosopagnosia are not always restricted to the perception of faces?

_C.K had severe object agnosia but could still see faces_

22. What is sound?

_vibrations of air molecules_

23. _Sound vibrations_

A: These are the physical factors that determine our perception of loudness, pitch, and timbre, respectively.

24. What is the difference between the tympanic membrane (ear drum) and the oval window?

_BOTH VIBRATE but the tympanic membranes vibrations are passed on to the ossicles whereas the oval windows is passed on to the choclea_

25. _ossicles_

A: These include the incus, malleus, and stapes.

26. What is the organ of Corti?

_membrane inside the choclea which is the auditory receptor organ includes 8 membranes itself. * basilor membrane (haircells) auditory receptors * tectoral rests on haircells_

27. How do hair cells transduce sound energy?

_Any type of deflection anywhere upon the organ of corti causes a force to be exerted on the haircells; the force then triggers an action potential in axons of the auditory nerve_

28.

A: This is called tonotopic organization!

_auditory system arrayed according to frequency_

Superior olives > inferior coliculi > medial genriculate nuclei > primary auditory cortex.

29. What is the function of the semicircular canals? they are the receptive organs of the vestibular system - carries information about direction and intensity of head movements, helps us maintain balance.

30. Primary auditory cortex    A: This is located in the lateral fissure.

31. What kinds of sounds are most effective at activating neurons in secondary auditory cortex? complex sound rather than pure

32. What two kinds of information are used to localize sounds in space? (lateral and medial superior olives)

33.    A: This animal is the barn owl.

34. What are the effects of auditory cortex damage? disrupt the ability to localize brief sounds and recognize rapid complex sequences of sound.

35. What are the three divisions of the somatosensory system? *exteroceptive - senses external stimuli applied to the skin *proprioceptive - monitors body position and movement. *interoceptive - monitors internal state

36. Proprioceptive    A: This is the somatosensory system involved in the perception of mechanical stimuli, thermal stimuli, and nociceptive stimuli.

37. What are the four types of cutaneous receptors?
FAST
  * free nerve endings - feel pain for extended periods
  * Pacinian corpuscles - high freqquency vibrations
  * Merkel's disks - indentation (pressure)
38. * Ruffini endings - skin stretch (gradual)    A: These sensations are mediated by free nerve endings.
  * hair follicule receptors - rapid speed (hair movement)
  * messiner corpuscles - low frequency vibration

Cutaneous pain, skin temp

39. *The identification of objects through touch.*    A: This ability is called stereognosis.

40. What is a dermatome?    *An area of the body that is innervated by the left and right dorsal roots of one segment of the spinal cord.*

41. Briefly describe the dorsal-column medial-lemniscus system pathway.    *Carries information about touch and proprioception enters spinal cord via a dorsal root > dorsal colum nuclei > decussate to medial lemniscus > ventral posterior thalamus > primary somatasensory cortex.*

42. *anterolateral system*    A: This exteroceptive somatosensory system carries information to the cortex about pain and temperature.

43.    A: These neurons would be the dorsal column neurons originating in the toes.

44. What are SI and SII?

45.    A: This is the trigeminal nerve (Cranial Nerve V).

46. Which thalamic areas would you lesion to reduce the deep, chronic pain associated with cancer? What about to sharp, acute pain?

47.    A: This is called somatotopic organization.

48. What is the homunculus?

49. Describe the location and organization of primary    *postcentral gyrus*
    somatosensory cortex.

50.                                         A: These would include the hands, lips, and tongue.

51. How many functional areas are there in SI? How are
    they organized?

52. What is the effect of somatosensory cortex damage in
    humans?

53.                                         A: This is called asomatognosia.

54. Extensive damage to the right posterior parietal lobe is
    associated with three neuropsychological deficits;
    identify each of these.

55. What is unusual about the cortical representation to
    pain?

56.                                         A: This is the anterior cingulate cortex.

57.                                         A: This is called the gate-control theory of pain.

58. Describe the role of the periaqueductal gray in the
    perception of pain.

59. What are endorphins?

60. What is phantom-limb pain?

61.                                          A: These include olfaction and gustation.

62. What is flavor?

63. What are pheromones?

64                                           A: This bone is called the cribriform plate.

65. What is noteworthy about the passage of olfactory signals from the olfactory bulb to cortical areas?

66. Describe the two major pathways of the olfactory system that leave the amygdala-piriform area.

67. What are the primary tastes?

68.                                          A: These would include the facial nerve (CN VII), the glossopharyngeal nerve (CN IX), and the vagus nerve (CN X).

69. How do the gustatory projections differ from those of the other sensory systems?

70. What is anosmia? How is it usually caused?

71. What is ageusia? What can cause ageusia for the anterior two-thirds of the tongue?

72.                                          A: This is called "selective attention".

73. What are the two key aspects of selective attention?

74. What are the two key mechanisms of selective attention?

75. What is "change blindness"?

76. What controls selective attention?

---

**Once you have completed the jeopardy study items, study them. Practice bidirectional studying; make sure that you know the correct answer to every question and the correct question for every answer.**

## II.    Essay Study Questions

*Using Chapter 8 of BIOPSYCHOLOGY, write an outline of the answer to each of the following essay study questions.*

1. Describe the dorsal and ventral visual pathways that transmit information from primary visual cortex to secondary visual and association cortices. Compare and contrast the "Where v. What" theory of dorsal v. ventral pathway function with the more recent "Behavioral Control v. Conscious Perception" theory.

2. Describe the functional organization of primary and secondary auditory cortex. Include details about the types of auditory stimuli you might use to maximize cell activity in specific areas of auditory cortex.

3. Compare and contrast the organization of the auditory system and the dorsal-column medial lemniscus sensory systems.

4. Describe the transmission of pain information through the anterolateral pathway, from nociceptors in the periphery to the perception of pain at the cortical level.

5. What are the three "paradoxes" of pain? Describe each of them

6. Describe the gate-control theory of pain and the evidence supporting this model.

7. Your friend was injured in a car accident and suffered extensive and irreparable damage to their primary visual cortex. However, you note that they still react to some visual stimuli; to what would you attribute this visual capacity? Describe the characteristics of this auxiliary visual system.

8. What is selective attention? Your description should include the two key aspects of selective attention, a consideration of top-down v. bottom-up levels of control, and an example of the effects of selective attention on behavior.

9. The chemical senses have several unique characteristics not shared by the senses of sight, touch or sound. Describe each of these characteristics and their possible functional significance.

When you have answered the essay study questions, memorize your outlines to prepare for your upcoming examination.

## III. Practice Examination

*After completing most of your studying of Chapter 8, but at least 24 hours before your formal examination, write the following practice examination.*

**A. Multiple-Choice Section.** Circle the correct answer for each question; *REMEMBER that some questions may have more than one correct answer.*

1. The flow of visual information goes from:

    a. primary visual cortex to prestriate cortex.
    b. prestriate cortex to posterior parietal cortex.
    c. prestriate cortex to inferotemporal cortex.
    d. posterior parietal cortex to inferotemporal cortex.

2. In human beings, most auditory cortex is in the depths of the:

    a. central fissure.
    b. lateral fissure.
    c. longitudinal fissure.
    d. occipital fissure.

3. Change blindness:

    a. exemplifies the effects of selective attention.
    b. is involved in the perception of rapid speech.
    c. is involved in the perception of sounds presented in rapid succession.
    d. is a phenomenon related to the fact that we typically form memories for only parts of a complex visual scene.

4. There are many opiate receptors in the:

    a. dorsal horns.
    b. dorsal-column medial-lemniscus system.
    c. PAG.
    d. raphé nucleus.

5. A pheromone is a:

    a. deficit in olfaction.
    b. chemical released by an animal that influences the behavior of its conspecifics.
    c. stimulus that elicits a conditioned taste aversion.
    d. fast-adapting cutaneous receptor.

6. The organ of Corti:

    a. contains the hair cells that transduce sound waves into sensation.
    b. is composed of the basilar membrane and the tectorial membrane.
    c. lies in the middle ear.
    d. carries information from the anterior two-thirds of the ipsilateral half of the tongue.

7. The dorsal pathway for projections from primary visual cortex:

    a. is responsible for conveying "what" information to inferotemporal cortex.
    b. is responsible for conveying information used to visually guide a person's behavior.
    c. projects to dorsal prestriate cortex and then to inferotemporal cortex.
    d. projects to dorsal prestriate cortex and then to posterior parietal cortex.

8. Prosopagnosia is:

    a. traditionally thought of as an inability to recognize faces.
    b. a general inability to recognize individual members of a class of visual stimuli.
    c. due to damage to striate cortex.
    d. due to damage to posterior parietal cortex.

9. Projections from the amygdala-pyriform area of the olfactory system:

    a. go to the thalamus and orbito-frontal cortex.
    b. go to the limbic system.
    c. convey information relevant to conscious perception of odors.
    d. convey information relevant to the emotional response to odors.

10. Selective attention is characterized by:

    a. the ability to restrict the flow of sensory information to your conscience.
    b. the ability to focus on all of the sensory stimuli that are present in your environment.
    c. unconscious monitoring of the environment for potentially relevant stimuli.
    d. increased blood flow to the secondary and association sensory cortices of the system under study.


**B. Modified True-False and Fill-in-the Blank Section.** If the statement is true, write TRUE in the blank provided. If the statement is false, write FALSE as well as the word or words that will make the statement true if they replaced the highlighted word or words in the original statement. If the statement is incomplete, write the word or words that will complete it.

1. **True or False: <u>Functional homogeneity</u>** characterizes the organization of sensory systems.

        A: _____

2. _____ are a product of the combined activity of the many cortical areas of each sensory system.

3. By definition, cortex that receives information from more than one sensory modality is called _____ cortex.

4. Cortically blind people can often provide information about visual stimuli (e.g., direction of movement) while claiming not to see anything; this phenomenon is called _____.

5. Many patients with extensive scotomas are unaware of them because of the phenomenon of _____.

6. **True or False:** A person who is unable to smell is suffering from **agnosia.**

   **A:** _____

7. An agnosia for faces is called _____.

8. The posterior parietal cortex is part of the _____ stream visual pathway.

9. The ability to subconsciously monitor the contents of several simultaneous conversations while attending consciously to another is called the _____ phenomenon.

10. **True or False:** The **President** is attached to the oval window.

    **A:** _____

11. Auditory hair cells are located on the _____ membrane of the organ of Corti.

12. The auditory system is organized _____, meaning that adjacent areas of cortex process adjacent sound frequencies.

13. Sounds are localized in space based upon differences in the perception of _____

    and of _____ between the two ears.

14. **True or False:** The **interoceptive system** is responsible for the perception of the position of various parts of the body on the basis of input from receptors in muscles and joints.

    **A:** _____

15. The ability to identify stimuli using only a sense of touch is called _____.

16. The largest, most deeply positioned cutaneous receptor is the _____ corpuscle.

17. Perception of both cutaneous pain and temperature is mediated by receptors called

    _____.

18. **True or False:** Patients with damage to SI and SII **cannot perceive** painful stimuli.

    **A:** _____

19. **True or False:** Lesions to the **ventral posterior nucleus** of the thalamus reduced deep chronic pain without disrupting cutaneous sensitivity.

    **A:** _____

20. Somatosensory information from the dorsal column nuclei ascend and decussate in the brainstem in a pathway called the _____.

21. The spinothalamic tract, the spinoreticular tract, and the spinotectal tract compose the

    _____ system.

22. SI is made up of a total of _____ independent parallel strips of cortical tissue that

    lie on the _____ gyrus of the parietal lobe.

23. The area of the body that is innervated by the left and right dorsal roots of a given segment of the spinal cord is

    called a _____.

24. _____ is the failure to recognize parts of one's own body.

25. Prefrontal _____ has been shown to reduce the emotional impact of pain, but it
    does not alter pain thresholds.

26. **True or False:** Neurons in the anterior portions of the auditory cortex respond specifically to **low-frequency**
    sounds.

        **A:** _____

27. The discovery of opiate receptors in the brain suggested that the body might be able to produce

    _____ opiates.

28. Patients lacking a sense of smell are said to be _____; those lacking a sense of

    taste are said to be _____.

29. Odoriferous chemicals released by an animal that influence the behavior of its conspecifics are called

    _____.

30. The axons of olfactory receptor cells enter the _____ through the cribriform
    plate.

31. All tastes can be produced by combinations of four component tastes: sweet, _____,

    _____, and _____.

32. The _____ nucleus in the thalamus relays both somatosensory and gustatory
    information.

33. The interactions between primary sensory cortex, secondary sensory cortex, and association cortex are

    governed by three principles: 1) _____; 2)

    _____; and 3) _____.

## C. Diagrams

**Figure 1.** Higher-Order Visual Pathways. Identify the 8 key areas of the cortical visual pathways.

A. _____

B. _____

C. _____

D. _____

E. _____

F. _____

G. _____

H. _____

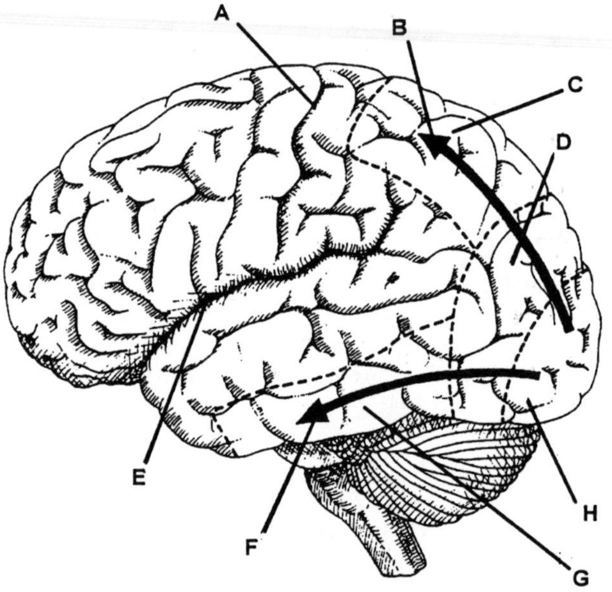

**Figure 2.** Identify the following 9 key areas of the anterolateral pain pathway and the descending pain control pathway originating in the PAG.

A. _____

B. _____

C. _____

D. _____

E. _____

F. _____

G. _____

H. _____

I. _____

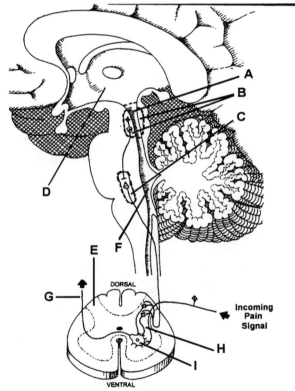

**D. Short Answer Section. In no more than 5 sentences, answer each of the following questions.**

1. Describe the location and function of the four main areas of the neocortex that are involved in vision.

2. How are sound waves transduced into auditory sensations? Describe this process, beginning with the arrival of sound waves at the tympanic membrane and ending with the conduction of action potentials by the auditory nerve.

3. The chemical senses participate in some interesting forms of learning; what are they?

---

**Mark your answers to the practice examination; the correct answers follow. On the basis of your performance, plan the final stages of your studying.**

# Answers to the Practice Examination

## A. Multiple Choice Section

1. a, b, c
2. b
3. a, d
4. a, c
5. b

6. a, b
7. b, d
8. a, b
9. a, b, c, d
10. a, c, d

## B. Modified True/False and Fill-in-the-Blank Section

1. False; functional segregation
2. Perceptions
3. association
4. blindsight
5. completion
6. False; anosmia
7. prosopagnosia
8. dorsal stream
9. cocktail
10. False; stapes
11. basilar
12. tonotopically
13. time of arrival; amplitude
14. False; proprioceptive
15. stereognosis
16. Pacinian
17. free nerve endings

18. False; can still feel
19. False; intralaminar and parafascicular nuclei
20. medial lemniscus
21. anterolateral pain/temperature
22. four; postcentral
23. dermatome
24. Asomatognosia
25. lobotomy
26. False; high-frequency
27. endogenous
28. anosmic; ageusic
29. pheromones
30. olfactory bulbs
31. salty; bitter; sour
32. ventral posterior
33. hierarchical organization; functional segregation; parallel processing

## C. Diagrams

**Figure 1.** A) Central Sulcus   B) Dorsal Pathway   C) Posterior Parietal Cortex   D) Prestriate Cortex   E) Lateral Sulcus   F) Ventral Pathway   G) Inferotemporal Cortex   H) Occipital Lobe

**Figure 2.** A) Cerebral Aqueduct   B) Periaqueductal Gray   C) Raphe Nucleus   D) Third Ventricle (Hypothalamus)   E) Dorsal Horn   F) Fourth Ventricle   G) Anterolateral Path   H) Interneurons   I) Second-Order Neurons

## D. Short Answer Section

1. Mention primary visual cortex (receives information from lateral geniculate nuclei of thalamus); prestriate cortex (secondary visual cortex; processes information from striate or primary visual cortex); posterior parietal cortex (the where/how system; the final region of the dorsal stream pathway); inferotemporal cortex (the what system; the final region of the ventral stream pathway).

2. Mention that sound waves cause the tympanic membrane to vibrate; this movement is transferred by the bones of the middle ear (malleus, incus and stapes) to the oval window, which transfers energy to fluid of inner ear; this sets up a "wave" along the organ of Corti; movement of hair cells on basilar membrane of organ of Corti leads generation of an action potential, which is carried into CNS by auditory nerve (CNVIII).

3. Mention conditioned taste aversions; conditioned taste preferences; odor-based feeding or copulatory preferences.

# Chapter 9

# THE SENSORIMOTOR SYSTEM

## I.    Jeopardy Study Items

*With reference to Chapter 9 of BIOPSYCHOLOGY, write the correct answer to each of the following questions and the correct question for each of the following answers.*

1.   Describe the hierarchical organization of the
      sensorimotor system.

2.   How is behavior affected by eliminating somatosensory
      feedback from the arms?

3.                                                    A: These are called ballistic movements.

4.   What cortical area is involved in integrating the original
      position of a limb and the location of external objects
      with which that limb will interact.

5.                                                    A: This area is called the posterior parietal cortex.

6.   Which sensory systems send information to the posterior
      parietal cortex?

7.                                        A: These are called the frontal eye fields.

8.   What is apraxia; what kinds of lesions produce it?

9.                                        A: This is called constructional apraxia.

10.   What is contralateral neglect; what kinds of lesions
       produce it?

11.                                     A: This is called the prefrontal cortex.

12.  Describe the connectivity of the dorsolateral prefrontal
       cortex.

13.                                     A: These are called memory fields.

14.  In general, what are the functions of dorsolateral
       prefrontal cortex in movement?

15.                                     A: These include the supplementary motor area, the
                                             premotor cortex, and the cingulate motor areas.

16.  How are areas of secondary motor cortex anatomically
       similar?

17. What do PET studies suggest about the function of
    secondary motor cortex?

18. How do the functions of supplementary motor cortex and
    premotor cortex differ?

19.                                    A: It is located on the precentral gyrus

20. What is the motor homunculus? What areas of the body
    are overrepresented?

21. What part of motor cortex controls the movement of
    individual fingers? How does this fact contradict
    Penfield's original notion of a motor homunculus?

22. What is stereognosis? What kind of sensory feedback
    underlies this ability?

23. What are the effects of damaging primary motor cortex?

24.                                    A: This is called astereognosia.

25. What is the sensorimotor function of the cerebellum and
    basal ganglia?

26. What anatomical evidence hints at the complexity of the
    cerebellum?

27. What are the effects of cerebellar damage?

28. Why do some people think that the basal ganglia are more complex than the cerebellum?

29.                                     A: This part of the brain receives input from the neocortex and transmits it back to various areas of motor cortex via the thalamus

30. How have theories of basal ganglia function recently changed?

31. Describe the dorsolateral corticospinal tract.

32.                                     A: These are called Betz cells.

33. What is unique about the dorsolateral corticospinal tract projections to the digits in primates?

34. What is the dorsolateral corticorubrospinal tract?

35.                                     A: This refers to the red nucleus of the midbrain.

36. Two motor pathways descend in the ventromedial portions of the spinal cord. What are the differences between them?

37.

A: These include the tectum, the vestibular nucleus, the reticular formation and the motor nuclei of the cranial nerves.

38. Compare and contrast the circuitry and targets of the dorsolateral and ventromedial motor pathways.

39. What was the effect of transecting the left and right dorsolateral corticospinal tracts in monkeys?

40.

A: This lesion induced severe postural abnormalities

41.

A: This is the only motor pathway capable of mediating independent movements of the digits.

42. What is the difference between a motor unit and a motor pool?

43.

A: This is called the neuromuscular junction.

44. What are the differences between fast muscle fibers and slow muscle fibers?

45.

A: These are called flexors.

46.

A: These are called antagonistic muscle groups.

47. What is the difference between dynamic contraction and isometric contraction?

Chapter 9

48. What are the main structural and functional differences
    between Golgi tendon organs and muscle spindles?

49. What is the purpose of intrafusal muscle?

50.                                              A: This is called the "patellar tendon" reflex.

51. What is a stretch reflex?

52. What is the day-to-day purpose of stretch reflexes?

53. What evidence suggests that the withdrawal reflex is not
    monosynaptic?

54.                                              A: This is called reciprocal innervation

55. What is a cocontraction? What is its functional
    significance to movement?

56.                                              A: It is mediated by Renshaw cells.

57. What evidence is there that the central motor programs
    for walking are in the spinal cord -- at least in cats?

58. What is a central sensorimotor program?

59. Describe Fentress' research that suggested that some fundamental central motor control programs are inherited.

60.                                          A: This is called response chunking.

61. What is a key principle of the chunking hypothesis of sensorimotor learning?

62. What are the two major advantages of shifting the level of control to lower levels of the sensorimotor system during sensorimotor learning?

---

**Once you have completed the jeopardy study items, study them. Practice bidirectional studying; make sure that you know the correct answer to every question and the correct question for every answer.**

## II.    Essay Study Questions

*Using Chapter 9 of BIOPSYCHOLOGY, write an outline of the answer to each of the following essay study questions.*

1. Pinel points out 3 key principles of sensorimotor function. Identify each of these, and provide an example from the text that illustrates each principle.

Chapter 9

2.  Describe the PET study of Jenkins and his colleagues, who examined the brain activity of humans as they
    learned to perform new motor sequences.  Include the six key findings of their work.

3.  Which are more devastating...lesions to primary motor cortex, or lesions to association cortices such as the
    posterior parietal lobe?  Support your answer with reference to research cited in your text.

4.  Compare and contrast the roles of the cerebellum and the basal ganglia on motor behavior.

5. Describe the structure and function of secondary motor cortices, including the newly-discovered cingulate motor areas.

6. Describe and interpret the classic studies of Lawrence and Kuypers, who examined the role of descending sensorimotor pathways on primate behavior.

7. There are two key areas of association cortex that influence sensorimotor function. Describe each of these areas, including their role in the initiation and control of movement.

Chapter 9

8.  Discuss the concept of central sensorimotor programs.  Include the role of response chunking and shifting control in the development of central sensorimotor programs.

9.  Describe the anatomy of the muscle spindle and its role in the patellar tendon reflex.

10.  Discuss the similarities between the organization and function of a big business and your sensorimotor system.

**When you have answered the essay study questions, memorize your outlines to prepare for your upcoming examination.**

## III.  Practice Examination

*After completing most of your studying of Chapter 9, but at least 24 hours before your formal examination, write the following practice examination.*

**A. Multiple-Choice Section.**  Circle the correct answer for each question; *REMEMBER that some questions may have more than one correct answer.*

1.  Which kinds of brain lesions are commonly associated with contralateral neglect?

    a.  bilateral frontal cortex lesions
    b.  left temporal cortex lesions
    c.  right posterior parietal cortex lesions
    d.  bilateral supplementary motor area lesions

2.  Which of the following areas of cortex is somatotopically organized?

    a.  primary motor cortex
    b.  supplementary motor cortex
    c.  premotor cortex
    d.  posterior parietal cortex

3.  Renshaw cells mediate:

    a.  cocontraction.
    b.  mutual inhibition.
    c.  lateral inhibition.
    d.  recurrent collateral inhibition.

4.  The advantages of cocontraction of antagonistic muscle groups include:

    a.  it makes movements quicker.
    b.  it makes movements smoother.
    c.  it insulates us from the effects of unexpected external forces.
    d.  it shifts responsibility for a movement to other muscle groups.

5.  Fentress (1973) showed that adult mice raised from birth without forelimbs:

    a.  still made the patterns of shoulder movements typical of grooming in their species.
    b.  made the tongue, head, and eye movements that would normally have occurred with specific shoulder movements in intact grooming mice.
    c.  would often interrupt ostensible grooming sequences to lick a cage mate.
    d.  "chunk" movements in a manner not observed in animals that have their forelimbs intact.

6.  During sensorimotor learning, there is a transfer of control from higher to lower sensorimotor circuits.  This transfer is advantageous because it:

    a.  frees the higher levels of the nervous system to deal with more complex issues.
    b.  increases the speed of movements.
    c.  increases conscious awareness of the response.
    d.  allows novel movements to be connected together.

7. In contrast to the descending ventromedial motor pathways, the dorsolateral motor pathways:

    a. control muscles capable of fine movements.
    b. control just one side of the body.
    c. are hierarchically organized.
    d. are chunked.

8. The primary motor cortex is:

    a. organized so that each area of the body is equally represented.
    b. organized somatotopically.
    c. the point of convergence of cortical sensorimotor signals.
    d. located in the parietal lobe.

9. Each skeletal muscle is:

    a. comprised of hundreds of thousands of muscle fibers.
    b. a flexor.
    c. usually comprised of fast-twitch fibers.
    d. synergistic.

10. Antagonistic muscles are:

    a. comprised of flexors and extensors that oppose one another's action at a joint.
    b. innervated by the same group of neurons.
    c. reciprocally innervated, so that when one contracts the other relaxes.
    d. essential to smooth movements, with the nature of the movement dependent upon adjustment in the level of relative cocontraction.

**B. Modified True-False and Fill-in-the Blank Section.** If the statement is true, write TRUE in the blank provided. If the statement is false, write FALSE as well as the word or words that will make the statement true if they replaced the highlighted word or words in the original statement. If the statement is incomplete, write the word or words that will complete it.

1. Most movements are guided by sensory feedback; however, _____ are not.

2. Many adjustments in motor output that occur in response to sensory feedback are unconsciously controlled by the _____ of the sensorimotor hierarchy.

3. Posterior parietal cortex is classified as _____ cortex because it receives sensory input from more than one sensory system.

4. **True or False:** Muscles that bend a joint are called **extensors.**

    **A:** _____

5. Although the symptoms of _____ are bilateral, it is often produced by unilateral damage to the left parietal lobe.

6. Patients with deficits on the block design subtest of the WAIS are said to suffer from

   _____.

7. **True or False:** The premotor cortex is considered to be **secondary motor cortex**.

   A: _____

8. **True or False:** According to the PET studies of Roland and his colleagues, there is **little activation** of secondary motor cortices when a simple motor task is performed.

   A: _____

9. The ventromedial-cortico-brainstem-spinal tract interacts with several brainstem nuclei; these include the _____, which receives auditory and visual information about spatial location, and the _____, which receives information about balance from the semicircular canals of the inner ear.

10. A _____ reflex is one that is elicited by a sudden lengthening of a muscle and its associated muscle spindles.

11. **True or False:** The **cerebellum** is involved in the modification of existing motor programs on the basis of sensory input.

    A: _____

12. The _____ receives most of the output of areas of secondary motor cortex.

13. Two muscles whose contraction produces the same joint movement are said to be _____; two whose contraction produces opposite joint movements are said to be _____.

14. **True or False:** A contraction that decreases muscle length is said to be an **isometric contraction**.

    A: _____

15. The proprioceptors in muscles are called _____; they are sensitive to the _____ of a muscle.

16. The proprioceptors that are located in tendons are called _____; they are sensitive to the _____ of the tendon due to muscular contractions.

17. **True or False:** Each muscle spindle contains a thread-like muscle called a **Golgi tendon organ.**

    A: _____

18. According to the _____ hypothesis of central motor programs, practice combines individual response elements into long sequences of behavior.

19. Which of the following statements is associated with the basal ganglia (BG), and which is associated with the cerebellum (C)?

   a) It comprises just 10% of the mass of the brain, but it contains more than 50% of its neurons.

   A: _____

   b) Diffuse damage here produces disturbances of balance, gait, speech, and eye movements.

   A: _____

   c) Diffuse damage here eliminates the ability to adapt motor output to changing conditions.

   A: _____

   d) This area receives input from various cortices and transmits it back to motor cortex via the thalamus.

   A: _____

   e) Damage to this "motor" system can also disrupt a variety of cognitive functions.

   A: _____

20. There are four major motor tracts that descend from the primary motor cortex to the spinal cord. Write the name of the tract associated with each of the following.

   a) red nucleus: _____ tract

   b) Betz cells: _____ tract

   c) Some axons in this tract synapse directly on motor neurons: _____ tract

   d) The axons in this tract synapse on interneurons that in turn synapse on motor neurons that project to the muscles of the arms and legs: _____ tract

   e) This pathway makes connections in the tectum, reticular formation, and vestibular nucleus:

   _____ tract

   f) The axons of this tract descend ipsilaterally from the primary motor cortex directly into the ventromedial spinal white matter: _____ tract

## Answers to Practice Examination

### A. Multiple Choice Section

| | | |
|---|---|---|
| 1. c | 5. a, b, c | 9. a |
| 2. a, b, c | 6. a, b | 10. a, c, d |
| 3. d | 7. a, b | |
| 4. b, c | 8. b, c | |

### B. Modified True/False and Fill-in-the-Blank Section

1. ballistic movements
2. spinal circuits
3. association
4. False; flexors
5. apraxia
6. constructional apraxia
7. True
8. False; extensive activation
9. tectum; vestibular nucleus
10. stretch
11. True
12. primary motor cortex
13. synergistic; antagonistic
14. False; dynamic contraction
15. Muscle spindles; length (stretch)

16. Golgi tendon organs; tension
17. False; intrafusal muscle fiber
18. chunking
19. a) cerebellum
    b) cerebellum
    c) cerebellum
    d) basal ganglia and basal ganglia
    e) cerebellum and basal ganglia
20. a) dorsolateral corticorubrospinal
    b) dorsolateral corticospinal
    c) dorsolateral corticospinal
    d) dorsolateral corticorubrospinal
    e) ventromedial cortico-brainstem-spinal
    f) ventromedial corticospinal

### C. Diagrams

**Figure 1.**

A) Supplementary Motor Cortex  B) Cingulate Motor Areas  C) Central Sulcus
D) Primary Motor Cortex (Precentral Gyrus)  E) Posterior Parietal Cortex
F) Dorsolateral Prefrontal Association Cortex  G) Premotor Cortex

**Figure 2.**

A) Primary Motor Cortex  B) Corticospinal Pathway  C) Pyramids  D) Corticorubrospinal Pathway
E) Red Nucleus  F) Brainstem Nuclei for Cranial Nerves  G) Ventral Horns of Spinal Cord

### D. Short Answer Section

1. Mention that muscle spindles are in the muscle whereas the GTO is located in the tendon; muscle spindles provide feedback about, and control, the length/stretch of a muscle, whereas the GTO monitors and controls the tension the muscle is placing on the tendon.

2. Mention chunking (programs for individual movements combined into novel, longer sequences) and changing levels of motor control (from cortex to brainstem/spinal circuitry; frees cortex for other tasks and speeds movement).

3. Mention that both have extensive reciprocal connectivity to motor cortex; that both lack direct connections to motor neurons, suggesting a modulatory role in the control of movement; cerebellum corrects movements that deviate from their intended course while basal ganglia modulate motor output; both are involved in various cognitive functions and sensorimotor learning.

```
┌─────────────────────────────────────────────────────────────┐
│ ┌─────────────────────────────────────────────────────────┐ │
│ │                                                         │ │
│ │                     Chapter 10                          │ │
│ │                                                         │ │
│ │              THE BIOPSYCHOLOGY OF                       │ │
│ │              EATING AND DRINKING                        │ │
│ │                                                         │ │
│ └─────────────────────────────────────────────────────────┘ │
└─────────────────────────────────────────────────────────────┘
```

## I.    Jeopardy Study Items

*With reference to Chapter 10 of BIOPSYCHOLOGY, write the correct answer to each of the following questions and the correct question for each of the following answers.*

1.                                             A:  This is called digestion.

2.  What are the three forms of energy that the body receives
    as a consequence of digestion?

3.  What are the three forms of energy that the body stores?

4.  Why is it more efficient for the body to store energy in
    the form of fat?

5.                                             A:  These are called the cephalic, absorptive, and fasting
                                                   phases of energy metabolism.

6.  Describe the role of insulin in the cephalic and
    absorptive phases of energy metabolism.

7.  Describe the role of glucagon in the fasting phase of energy metabolism.

8.                                          A: This is called gluconeogenesis.

9.                                          A: This is used by muscles as a fuel source during the fasting phase of energy metabolism.

10. What three components are shared by all set-point systems?

11.                                         A: This is called a negative feedback system.

12. What were the two set-point theories of hunger and feeding that evolved in the 1940s and 1950s?

13. From an evolutionary perspective, what is wrong with set-point theories of hunger and feeding?

14.                                         A: These factors include taste, learning, and social influences.

15. What is the key idea behind the positive-incentive theory of feeding?

16. According to the positive-incentive theory of feeding, what factors determine the amount that we eat?

17. Why do most humans prefer sweet, salty or fatty foods?

18. What is a conditioned taste aversion?

19. Why is it often difficult to consume a balanced diet in today's "fast-food" society?

20. What kinds of factors determine the frequency with which a person will eat?

21. According to Woods, what is the cause of premeal hunger?

22.                                          A: This is called the nutritive density of food.

23. What is sham eating? What does it indicate about satiety mechanisms?

24.                                          A: This is called the "appetizer effect".

25. How do social factors alter food intake in human beings?

26.                                    A: This is called a cafeteria diet.

27. What effect does the number of flavors available at a
    meal have on feeding behavior? Why?

28. Describe the phenomenon of sensory-specific satiety.

29. What are two adaptive consequences of sensory-specific
    satiety?

30. Why do blood glucose levels often drop just before a
    meal?

31. What effects do large, bilateral lesions of the
    ventromedial region of the hypothalamus have on the
    feeding behavior of rats?

32.                                    A: This is called hyperphagia.

33.                                    A: These stages are called the static and dynamic phases.

34. What happens to the body weight of VMH-lesioned rats
    during the static phase of the lesion's effects?

35. When do VMH-lesioned rats tend to eat less than
    unlesioned control rats?

36. What effects do large, bilateral lesions of the lateral hypothalamus have on the feeding behavior of rats?

37. Why do VMH lesions cause such large weight gains in rats?

38.                                    A: These are called lipogenesis and lipolysis, respectively.

39. Damage to which two structures can produce hyperphagia that is similar to that attributed to VMH lesions?

40. What evidence indicates that signals from the stomach are not necessary for hunger or for body weight regulation?

41. How did Koopmans' "stomach transplant" study support the idea that the stomach has some role in satiety and feeding?

42.                                    A: This peptide is called cholecystokinin.

43. Where are the CCK receptors that mediate the peptide's effect on feeding behavior located? What does this suggest about their satiety-inducing effects?

44.                                    A: These peptides include neuropeptide Y and galanin.

45. How stable is an adult's body weight? What does this suggest about a set-point model of feeding?

46.                                    A: This means free-feeding.

47. What is the relationship between body weight and energy utilization?

48. Describe the beneficial effects of dietary restriction.

49.                                        A: This is called diet-induced thermogenesis.

50. What is the key difference between a set-point and a settling point?

51.                                        A: This is called lipectomy.

52.                                        A: This compartment includes the interstitial fluid, the blood, and the cerebrospinal fluid.

53.                                        A: This is called an isotonic solution.

54. What is osmotic pressure?

55. What organ regulates the body's water and sodium balance?

56.                                        A: This is called a nephron.

57. List five ways that the body could lose water.

58. How does the body react to a decrease in its water resources?

59.                                              A: This is called hypovolemia.

60. What is the difference between hypovolemia and cellular
    dehydration?

61. Why do salty foods make you thirsty?

62. How is cellular dehydration induced in experimental
    subjects so that its effects can be studied independently
    of hypovolemia?

63.                                              A: These are called osmoreceptors.

64. How do osmoreceptors induce thirst?

65. How is hypovolemia induced in experimental animals so
    that its effects can be studied independently of cellular
    dehydration?

66.                                              A: These are called baroreceptors and blood flow receptors.

67. What is antidiuretic hormone?

68. What is the relation between renin, angiotensin II, and
    aldosterone?

69.                                              A: This is called a dipsogen.

70. What suggested that the subfornical organ might play a role in angiotensin-II's dipsogenic effect?

71. What suggests that drinking in response to naturally occurring water deficits is primarily the result of cellular dehydration?

72.                                          A: This is called spontaneous drinking.

73. How is insulin related to both feeding and drinking behavior?

74.                                          A: This is called the saccharin elation effect

75.    What is schedule-induced polydipsia?

76. Why have evolutionary factors contributed to the problem of obesity?

77. What is leptin? What does it tell us about obesity?

78. What is the key difference between anorexia nervosa and bulimia nervosa?

Once you have completed the jeopardy study items, study them. Practice bidirectional studying; make sure that you know the correct answer to every question and the correct question for every answer.

## II.    Essay Study Questions

*Using Chapter 10 of BIOPSYCHOLOGY, write an outline of the answer to each of the following essay study questions.*

1.  Describe that various factors that influence spontaneous drinking.

2.  Summarize the hypothalamic set-point model of the physiology of eating, which was dominant in the 1950s and 1960s.  On what findings was the model based?

3.  Describe and critically evaluate the idea that increases and decreases from an internal set point (for blood glucose or for body fat) are critical factors in satiety and hunger, respectively.

4.  What evidence suggests that there is a gastrointestinal peptide satiety signal?

5.  How has the view of the role of the hypothalamus in eating changed since the 1950s? Specifically, how have the hyperphagia and obesity produced by large bilateral VMH lesions and the cessation of feeding produced by LH lesions been reinterpreted?

6.  Describe some of the factors that influence when we eat and how much we eat.

Chapter 10

7.  The idea that eating is a response to energy deficits has been replaced by positive-incentive theories of feeding. Describe this theory and explain why it has replaced the idea of feeding as a response to energy deficits.

8.  What is the settling-point (leaky-barrel) model of the regulation of ingestive behaviors? Contrast it with the set-point (thermostat) model.

9.  Describe the evidence that supports the idea that the lateral preoptic area and the subfornical organ play key roles in the regulation of drinking behavior.

10. Describe the compensatory events that are triggered by a decrease in blood pressure and blood flow.

11. Most of the drinking that we do is spontaneous drinking, yet most the research on the physiology of drinking has focused on drinking induced by cellular dehydration or hypovolemia. Discuss.

12. Describe the symptoms and prognosis of anorexia nervosa.

13. Describe the three phases of energy metabolism and their control by the pancreatic hormones insulin and glucagon.

14. Discuss the neural bases for drinking behavior induced by hypovolemia and cellular dehydration, respectively.

15. "Obesity is the product of evolution gone awry".   Discuss this statement and its implications for how obesity is viewed and treated.

---

**When you have answered the essay study questions, memorize your outlines to  prepare for your upcoming examination.**

---

## III.   Practice Examination

After completing most of your studying of Chapter 10, but at least 24 hours before your formal examination, write the following practice examination.

**A. Multiple-Choice Section.** Circle the correct answer for each question; *REMEMBER that some questions may have more than one correct answer.*

1.  In rats, bilateral LH lesions produce:

    a. aphagia.
    b. adipsia.
    c. apraxia.
    d. agnosia.

2.  Insulin and glucagon are synthesized and released by the:

    a. liver.
    b. duodenum.
    c. pancreas.
    d. kidney.

3.  During the fasting phase, the body (excluding the brain) obtains most of its energy from:

    a. glucose.
    b. free fatty acids.
    c. ketones.
    d. glycogen

4.  According to Woods, the key to understanding hunger is:

    a. understanding the idea of set-points.
    b. understanding why glucose is present in the cerebrospinal fluid.
    c. understanding that feeding stresses the body.
    d. understanding that hunger pangs are not signaling a need for food, they represent your body's preparations for an expected meal.

5.  Koopmans implanted an extra stomach into rats. He found:

    a. that a gastric satiety factor was being released from the implant into the blood.
    b. that injections of food into the implanted stomach reduced food consumption.
    c. that neural signals play an important role in eating.
    d. that infusion of glucose into the bloodstream increased the contractions in both stomachs.

6.  Bilateral VMH lesions increase:

    a. lipogenesis.
    b. lipolysis.
    c. eating.
    d. drinking

7. The evidence suggests that the hyperphagia produced by large bilateral VMH lesions is:

    a. unrelated to the weight gain.
    b. to a large degree a secondary consequence of an increase in lipogenesis.
    c. to a large degree a secondary consequence of an increase in lipolysis.
    d. caused by hypoinsulemia.

8. In the first part of an important experiment by Weingarten, a buzzer-and-light conditional stimulus was presented before each meal. In the second part of this experiment:

    a. the conditional stimulus was shown to decrease eating.
    b. the conditional stimulus caused the rats to start eating, even if they had just finished eating a meal.
    c. feeding behavior was found to be extinguished.
    d. the conditional stimulus had become an extinguished stimulus.

9. Which of the following is the basis for a mammal's ability to select a healthy combination of foods in its natural environment?

    a. a preference for sweet tastes
    b. a preference for salty tastes
    c. a mechanism that increases salt preference when there is a sodium deficiency
    d. the ability for the consequences of ingestion (good or bad) to influence the incentive value of a food's taste and thus its subsequent consumption.

10. The peptide CCK may reduce feeding behavior by:

    a. increasing the absorption of food from the duodenum.
    b. altering the release of insulin from the hypothalamus.
    c. altering neural activity in the CNS.
    d. slowing the release of food from the stomach.

11. Osmotic pressure draws:

    a. water from hypertonic solutions.
    b. water from hypotonic solutions.
    c. solutes from hypertonic solutions.
    d. solutes from hypotonic solutions.

12. The fact that small iv injections of hypertonic saline into a carotid artery can elicit drinking suggests that there are:

    a. blood-flow receptors in the brain.
    b. blood-pressure receptors in the brain.
    c. osmoreceptors in the brain.
    d. blood-pressure receptors in the carotid artery.

13. Nicolaidis and Roland (1975) added quinine to the drinking water of rats. This:

    a. increased the amount that the rats drank.
    b. decreased the amount that the rats drank.
    c. increased the body weight of the rats.
    d. led to several deaths from dehydration.

14. Which of the following is often a symptom of anorexia nervosa?

    a. weight loss
    b. hyperphagia
    c. unrealistic body image
    d. increased pleasure from food

15. People who are not anorectic but who display recurring cycles of bingeing, purging, and fasting are said to suffer from:

    a. hyperphagia.
    b. anorexia nervosa.
    c. hypophagia.
    d. bulimia nervosa.

16. People who suffer from obesity:

    a. will lose weight on a long-term basis only if they adopt permanent lifestyle changes.
    b. have an imbalance between energy intake and energy expenditures.
    c. can lose significant amounts of weight by doing nothing more than exercising.
    d. have no control over their behavior.

17. Sensory-specific satiety is an important factor in gustatory behavior because it:

    a. ensures that we do not eat too much.
    b. encourages animals to eat different types of food and thus consume a balanced diet.
    c. encourages animals to eat many different foods during times of food abundance.
    d. maintains our interest in food.

18. Animals with lesions of the LH may cease eating because of:

    a. unintended damage to areas such as the dorsal noradrenergic bundle.
    b. increased blood insulin levels and the resulting lipogenesis.
    c. generalized deficits in motor and sensory function.
    d. cells that respond to the incentive properties of food.

19. Canon and Washburn's report that hunger is due to stomach contractions was:

    a. based on Washburn's introspections and his ability to swallow a balloon.
    b. disproved when it was shown that surgical removal of the stomach did not eliminate hunger pangs.
    c. supported by Koopmans' "stomach transplant" studies.
    d. disproved by the effect that CCK has on feeding behavior.

20. Drinking behavior:

    a. is less important than feeding behavior to short-term survival.
    b. that is produced by naturally occurring deficits is most likely a response to cellular dehydration
    c. is not generally affected by factors such as flavor or food.
    d. normally occurs in the absence of any deficit.

21. Feeding and drinking behaviors can both be affected by:

    a. lesions of the LH.
    b. learning.
    c. flavor.
    d. alterations in their set points.

22. The subfornical organ:

    a. plays a key role in gustatory behaviors.
    b. plays a key role in drinking behavior elicited by bloodborne angiotensin II.
    c. plays a key role in drinking behavior elicited by centrally released angiotensin II.
    d. releases the transmitter acetylcholine to mediate its effects on drinking behavior.

23. Injections of galanin or neuropeptide Y into the paraventricular nucleus of the hypothalamus elicits:

    a. a significant increase in all gustatory behavior.
    b. a significant decrease in all gustatory behavior.
    c. a significant increase in the ingestion of carbohydrates or fats, respectively.
    d. a significant increase in the ingestion of fats or carbohydrates, respectively.

24. Animals who have their food intake restricted to levels 30%-60% of free-feeding control animals:

    a. lost a potentially fatal amount of weight.
    b. are likely to develop adipsia.
    c. live longer, healthier lives.
    d. live shorter though healthier lives.

25. Decreasing a person's food intake:

    a. will decrease the efficiency with which they utilize the food that they do consume.
    b. is a good way to reduce their body weight.
    c. will increase the efficiency with which they utilize the food that they do consume.
    d. will reset their body fat set point.


**B. Modified True-False and Fill-in-the Blank Section.** If the statement is true, write TRUE in the blank provided. If the statement is false, write FALSE as well as the word or words that will make the statement true if they replaced the highlighted word or words in the original statement. If the statement is incomplete, write the word or words that will complete it.

1. The _____ phase of feeding may begin with the smell, sight, or simple thought of food.

2. **True or False:** Injections of water into the **ventricles** of water-deprived rats reduces drinking when these rats are given free access to water.

    **A:** _____

3. Drinking in the absence of deficits is called _____.

4. The calories contained in a given volume of food reflects the _____ of that food.

5. The early theory that signals from the _____ play a critical role in hunger and satiety was abandoned when it was noted that surgical removal of this organ did not eliminate hunger pangs.

6. In a _____ feeding experiment, food that is eaten never reaches the stomach because it passes out of the body through an tube implanted in the esophagus.

7. Many studies of feeding have been based on the premise that eating is controlled by a system designed to maintain the homeostasis of the body's energy resources by responding to deviations from a hypothetical _____.

8. The body has three sources of energy:  glucose, _____, and _____.

9. Excessive drinking caused by the presentation of food on an intermittent basis is called _____.

10. **True or False:** Sensory-specific satiety helps to **restrict** the variety of foods that an animals will eat.

   **A:** _____

11. The point made by the saccharin elation effect is that drinking a beverage temporarily _____ the incentive value of similar-tasting beverages.

12. Presenting a rat with a different-tasting palatable solution every 15 minutes will induce _____ in most subjects.

13. _____ causes the kidney to absorb much of the sodium that would otherwise have been lost in the urine.

14. According to the pre-eminent theory of the 1950s and 60s, the _____ nucleus of the hypothalamus is a feeding center, and the _____ nucleus is a satiety center.

15. The syndrome produced by bilateral VMH lesions in rats has two phases: the _____ phase is first and the _____ phase is second.

16. The role played by taste in the development of satiety is illustrated by the phenomenon of _____ satiety, in which eating a food may produce satiety for the taste of that food while having little effect on the incentive properties of other tastes.

Chapter 10

17. There are three stages of metabolism associated with a meal; in chronological order, these are:

    a.    the _____ phase

    b.    the _____ phase

    c.    the _____ phase

18. Osmoreceptors appear to be located in the _____ nucleus of the hypothalamus.

19. Insulin is released during the cephalic and _____ phases of metabolism, and glucagon is released during the _____ phase.

20. During starvation the brain receives its energy from _____ , which are breakdown products of body fat.

21. As an individual gains weight, there is often an increase in his or her body temperature that counteracts further weight gain by wasting calories. Such an increase in body temperature is commonly referred to as _____ thermogenesis.

22. Bombesin, glucagon, somatostatin, and _____ are peptide hormones that are released by the gastrointestinal tract and have been shown to reduce food intake.

23. Evidence suggests that the hyperphagia that is produced by large bilateral lesions to the VMH is caused in part by damage to the _____ nuclei of the hypothalamus or their connections.

24. In _____ drinking experiments, the water that a subject drinks flows down its esophagus and out of its body before it can be absorbed.

25. Two-thirds of the body's water is located _____.

26. **True or False:** Animals that are deficient in **a vitamin or mineral** have to learn which foods contain the vitamin or mineral.

        **A:** _____

27. Obese individuals may have an enhanced cephalic-phase secretion of _____, which would cause them to store a disproportionate amount of food as fat.

28. Osmoreceptors respond to cellular dehydration by eliciting the perception of thirst and by releasing the hormone _____.

29. _____ are glue-like substances with molecules much too large to pass through cell membranes.

30. Both ADH and the activity of blood-flow receptors in the kidneys cause the kidneys to release
    _____, and this causes the formation of the peptide dipsogen, _____.

31. **True or False:** The release of <u>**glucagon**</u> causes the kidneys to reabsorb more sodium.

    **A:** _____

32. Cerebral angiotensin II receptors are located in the _____ of the brain.

33. Angiotensin II produces an increase in blood pressure by constricting peripheral blood vessels and by
    triggering the release of _____ from the adrenal cortex.

34. **True or False:** High <u>**cholecystokinin**</u> levels stimulate the formation of ketones from free fatty acids.

    **A:** _____

35. Fat is the most efficient form of energy storage because a gram of fat holds _____ as
    many calories as a gram of glycogen, and fat does not absorb _____.

Chapter 10

## C. Diagrams.

**Figure 1.** The Diencephalon and Ingestive Behaviors. Identify the structures highlighted in the diagram, including the 5 diencephalic structures that have been implicated as playing a role in ingestive behavior.

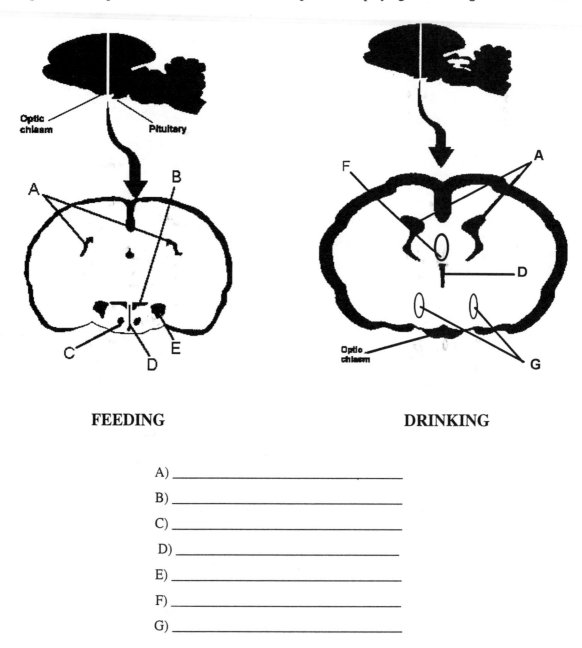

**FEEDING**                    **DRINKING**

A) _____

B) _____

C) _____

D) _____

E) _____

F) _____

G) _____

166

**D. Short Answer Section.** In no more than 5 sentences, answer each of the following questions.

1. Briefly describe how differences in energy intake, storage or expenditure could conspire to produce a state of obesity.

2. Point out the flaws with the statement "You drink when you feel thirsty".

3. Signals from the stomach have long been believed to play a role in the cessation of feeding behavior. Discuss this research, including its historical basis and current thinking in the area.

Chapter 10

4. How do osmoreceptors induce drinking behavior?

5. Many college students who live in dormitories find that they gain weight; given what you know about gustatory behavior, why should this be so?

6. What evidence suggests that VMH lesions elicit feeding by a mechanism other than the destruction of a "satiety center" in the brain.

**Mark your answers to the practice examination; the correct answers follow. On the basis of your performance, plan the final stages of your studying.**

## Answers to Practice Examination

### A. Multiple Choice Section

| | | | | |
|---|---|---|---|---|
| 1. a, b | 6. a, c | 11. b | 16. a, b | 21. a, b, c |
| 2. c | 7. b | 12. c | 17. b, c | 22. b |
| 3. b, c | 8. b | 13. b | 18. c | 23. d |
| 4. c, d | 9. a, b, c, d | 14. a, c | 19. a, b | 24. c |
| 5. a, b | 10. c, d | 15. d | 20. b, d | 25. c |

### B. Modified True/False and Fill-in-the-Blank.

1. cephalic
2. False; bloodstream
3. spontaneous drinking
4. nutritive density
5. stomach
6. sham
7. set point
8. lipids; amino acids
9. schedule-induced polydipsia
10. False; increase
11. reduces
12. polydipsia
13. aldosterone
14. lateral; ventromedial
15. dynamic; static
16. sensory-specific satiety
17. cephalic; absorptive; fasting
18. supraoptic nucleus
19. absorptive; fasting
20. ketones
21. diet-induced thermogenesis
22. cholecyctokinin
23. paraventricular nucleus
24. sham
25. intracellularly
26. True
27. insulin
28. ADH
29. Colloids
30. renin; angiotensin II
31. aldosterone
32. subfornical organ
33. aldosterone
34. False; glucagon
35. twice; water

### C. Diagrams

**Figure 1.** A) Lateral Ventricles  B) Paraventricular Nucleus  C) Ventromedial Nucleus  D) Third Ventricle  E) Lateral Hypothalamus  F) Subfornical Organ  G) Supraoptic Nuclei

### D. Short Answer Section

1. Mention that hyperinsulinemia or exaggerated cephalic-phase insulin release can produce excessive lipogenesis; that metabolic efficiency can differ greatly between individuals, resulting in differential weight gain with identical diets.

2. Mention that most drinking is spontaneous; that drinking is greatly affected by flavor, the presence of food, and learning; animals usually drink in excess of their needs.

3. Mention the classic balloon-swallowing experiments of Canon and Washburn; how their theory was cast into doubt by the effects of stomach removal on hunger; how Koopmans' work on transplanted stomachs has revived this idea, suggesting that a blood-borne signal plays a role in satiety.

4. Mention their direct stimulation of drinking via activation of neural circuits and their indirect stimulation of drinking through the release of ADH.

5. Mention the factors that would encourage excessive eating: cafeteria-style diet; regularly scheduled meals; eating with other people.

6. Mention the lesion-induced hyperinsulinemia that causes VMH lesioned rats to store more fat than unlesioned controls eating the same amount of food; that the effects of lesions in the area of the VMH appear to be due to accidental damage to nearby structures such as the dorsal noradrenergic bundle or the paraventricular nucleus of the hypothalamus.

## Chapter 11

## HORMONES AND SEX

## I.    Jeopardy Study Items

*With reference to Chapter 11 of BIOPSYCHOLOGY, write the correct answer to each of the following questions and the correct question for each of the following answers.*

1. What is the "mamawawa" approach to studying sex and hormones?

2.                                          A: These are called endocrine glands.

3. What is a hormone?

4.                                          A: These are hormones that are synthesized from cholesterol.

5.                                          A: These are called testes or ovaries, respectively.

6. What is copulation?

7.                                          A: This is called a zygote.

8. What are the two main classes of gonadal hormones?

9. What are gonadotropins?

10. The pituitary comprises two independent endocrine
    glands; what are they, and where do they come from?

11. What is the major difference between the pattern of
    gonadal hormone release in males and females?

12.                                         A: This is the neural structure that controls the anterior
                                               pituitary.

13.                                         A: These are called vasopressin and oxytocin.

14. What are neurosecretory cells?

15. What is the hypothalamopituitary portal system?

16. What is a releasing factor?

17. How was thyrotropin- releasing hormone first isolated?

171

18. What is the difference between a releasing factor and a
    releasing hormone?

19.                                                   A: These are called FSH and LH, respectively.

20. What is ovulation?

21. When is a shift of control from a negative feedback
    system to a positive feedback system important in the
    release of gonadotropins?

22. What is one consequence of pulsatile hormone release?

23. What is a primordial gonad?

24. How does H-Y antigen control the differentiation of the
    primordial gonads?

25.                                        A: These are called the seminal vesicles and vas deferens.

26.                                        A: These are called the uterus and the fallopian tubes.

27. How do androgens and Müllerian-inhibiting substance
    control the differentiation of the internal reproductive
    ducts in males?

28. What are the differences among castration,
    gonadectomy, orchidectomy, and ovariectomy?

29. What is a *bipotential precursor?*

30. What controls the development of male and female
    external reproductive organs?

31. Describe some of the anatomical differences between
    the brains of men and women.

32. Why are rats convenient subjects for studying the effects
    of hormones on brain development?

33. What did early gonadal transplantation research suggest
    about the role of testosterone in sexual differentiation?

34. What does perinatal mean?

35. What evidence supports the hypothesis that aromatization
    plays a critical role in the sexual differentiation of the
    rat brain?

36.                                    A:  This is called *alpha fetoprotein.*

37.                                    A: These behaviors include mounting, intromission, and
                                       ejaculation.


38. What is lordosis?



39.                                    A: These are called secondary sex characteristics.



40. The levels of which hormones increase during puberty?



41.                                    A: This anterior pituitary hormone does not target an organ;
                                       instead, it acts directly on bone and muscle.



42. What is androstenedione?



43. What are the symptoms of androgenic insensitivity in
    genetic males?



44.                                    A: This syndrome is caused by a deficiency in the release of
                                       cortisol, which results in the release of high levels of adrenal
                                       androgens.



45. What happens to genetic adrenogenital females at
    puberty if they are not treated?



46. Why is the effectiveness of the sex-change operation
    that Money performed on his famous *ablatio-penis* twin
    controversial?

47. How effective is orchidectomy at reducing male sexual behavior?

48. What are the effects of testosterone replacement injections in adult males?

49.

A: This time period is called *estrus*.

50 What effect does ovariectomy have on women?

51. What controls the sex drive of human females?

52. What is an anabolic steroid?

53. What effects do high doses of anabolic steroids have on sexual behavior in men and women?

54.

A: This is also called the *sexually dimorphic nucleus*.

55. Which hormone influences the development of the sexually dimorphic nucleus of the hypothalamus?

56.

A: This is the brain area that seems to play a key role in male sexual behaviors like mounting.

57. What is the lateral tegmental field? What role does it play in male sexual behavior?

58. Which area of the hypothalamus is critical for the sexual behavior of female rats?

59. What is the periaqueductal gray? What role does it play in female sexual behavior?

60. What evidence is there that sexual preference has a genetic basis?

61.                                          A: This gene is located near the end of the X-chromosome.

62. What effect does hormone replacement have on sexual preference in orchidectomized males?

63. How do perinatal hormones influence the development of sexual preference?

64                                           A: These hormones seem to play a role in the development of sexual attraction.

65.                                          A: This area of the hypothalamus is called INAH 3.

66. What were the results of LeVay's (1991) study of brain structure and male homosexuality?

---

**Once you have completed the jeopardy study items, study them. Practice bidirectional studying; make sure that you know the correct answer to every question and the correct question for every answer.**

## II.    Essay Study Questions

*Using Chapter 11 of BIOPSYCHOLOGY, write an outline to answer to each of the following essay study questions.*

1.  Describe the different ways in which the anterior and posterior lobes of the pituitary gland are controlled by the hypothalamus.

2.  What are releasing hormones?  Provide two examples of a releasing hormone and its role in sexual behavior.

3.  Summarize the factors that control the differentiation of the gonads, the internal reproductive ducts, and the external reproductive organs.

4. "We are all genetically programmed to develop female bodies; genetic males develop male bodies only if their fundamentally female program of development is overruled by gonadal hormones". Explain and discuss this statement.

5. What is the *aromatization hypothesis* of the role of gonadal hormones in the sexual differentiation of the brain? What evidence suggests that aromatization is critical for the normal development of the male rat brain?

6. What parts of the hypothalamus seem to control sexual behavior in males? in females?

7.  What effects do hormones have on the development of secondary sex characteristics?

8.  Describe the androgenic insensitivity syndrome.  What does it indicate about the role of androgens in sexual development?

9.  What is the adrenogenital syndrome?  How is it treated?  What are the consequences of nontreatment?

10. Describe Money's famous and controversial treatment of the identical twin suffering from *ablatio penis*. What does it suggest about the role of social factors in sexual development? What does it suggest about science?

11. What are the effects of orchidectomy and/or testosterone injections on sexual behavior in adult human males? Compare these effects to the effect of ovariectomy on sexual behavior in adult female humans.

12. Describe the major difference between men and women in their patterns of gonadal hormone release. What evidence suggested that a difference in neural control, as opposed to differences between the anterior pituitaries of males and females, underlies the differences in hormone release.

13. Describe the effects of perinatal exposure to testosterone on the development of sexual behavior in males and females.

14. Describe the recent research on the relation between hypothalamic structure, gender, and sexual preference.

15. What are the differences between amino-acid derivative hormones, peptide hormones, and steroid hormones. Give an example of each class of hormone.

**When you have answered the essay study questions, memorize your outlines to prepare for your upcoming examination.**

## III.    Practice Examination

> *After completing most of your studying of Chapter 11, but at least 24 hours before your formal examination, write the following practice examination.*

**A.  Multiple-Choice Section.**  Circle the correct answer for each question; *REMEMBER that some questions may have more than one correct answer.*

1.  The two general types of glands in the body include the:

    a.  exocrine glands
    b.  pituitary glands
    c.  adrenal glands
    d.  endocrine glands

2.  Every cell in the normal human body, with the exception of some sperm cells, have:

    a.  23 chromosomes.
    b.  at least one Y chromosome.
    c.  at least one X chromosome.
    d.  a pair of X chromosomes.

3.  Tropic hormones:

    a.  are released from the anterior pituitary.
    b.  influence the release of hormones from other glands.
    c.  are released into the circulatory system.
    d.  regulate gonadal hormone release.

4.  Which of the following are hormones?

    a.  acetylcholine
    b.  epinephrine
    c.  cholesterol
    d.  estrogen

5.  Gonadotropin-releasing hormone directly stimulates the release of:

    a.  estrogen.
    b.  lutenizing hormone.
    c.  follicle stimulating hormone.
    d.  oxytocin.

6.  Feedback in the neuroendocrine system is:

    a.  usually negative.
    b.  usually positive.
    c.  always negative.
    d.  always positive.

7. Positive feedback plays an important role in:

    a. triggering ovulation.
    b. triggering puberty.
    c. triggering sexual preferences.
    d. triggering lordosis.

8. Behaviors by which females "solicit" males are called:

    a. naughty.
    b. lordotic.
    c. proceptive.
    d. receptive.

9. Orchidectomizing male rats shortly after birth:

    a. masculinizes their adult copulatory behavior.
    b. feminizes their adult copulatory behavior.
    c. demasculinizes their adult copulatory behavior.
    d. has no effect on their adult copulatory behavior.

10. The anterior pituitary gland:

    a. is directly connected to axons in the hypothalamus.
    b. is embryologically related to the tissue in the roof of the mouth.
    c. is connected to the hypothalamus via the circulatory system.
    d. releases tropic hormones.

11. Which sex chromosomes are possessed by somebody suffering from androgenic insensitivity syndrome?

    a. XY
    b. XX
    c. YY
    d. X

12. Which of the following is responsible for the pubertal feminization of androgen-insensitive males?

    a. androgens
    b. estrogens
    c. androstenedione
    d. progesterone

13. Money's famous patient suffering from ablatio penis was treated by:

    a. castrating him.
    b. giving him estrogen injections at puberty.
    c. raising him as a girl.
    d. creating an artificial vagina.

14. Orchidectomy produces a decline in the interest in reproductive behavior and in the ability to engage in it. However:

    a. the rate of the decline varies markedly from woman to woman.
    b. the rate of the decline varies markedly from man to man.
    c. it does not change a person's sexual preferences.
    d. adrenal androgens may maintain sexual behavior in some men.

15. Although orchidectomy eventually eliminates reproductive behavior in virtually all cases, there is:

    a. strong evidence of a correlation between sex drive and testosterone levels in healthy males.
    b. no strong evidence of a correlation between sex drive and testosterone levels in healthy males.
    c. no evidence that replacement injections can bring it back.
    d. evidence that this change may simply represent a new interest in horticulture.

16. Which of the following statements about estradiol and female sexual behavior is/are NOT TRUE?

    a. estradiol makes cells in the hypothalamus insensitive to progesterone
    b. estradiol increases the number of progesterone receptors in the ventromedial nucleus of the
hypothalamus
    c. estradiol enters cells in the ventromedial nucleus of the hypothalamus and influences gene expression
    d. injections of estradiol an progesterone into the ventromedial nucleus of the hypothalamus induce estrus
       in ovariectomized female rats

17. The sexually dimorphic nucleus is:

    a. located in the hypothalamus.
    b. larger in females than males.
    c. critically important to male sexual behavior.
    d. insensitive to the effects of testosterone.

18. Evidence that differences in sexual orientation have a genetic basis include the observation(s) that

    a. the concordance rate for homosexuality in monozygotic twins is much higher than for dizygotic twins.
    b. the concordance rate for male homosexuality in dizygotic twin brother is 100%.
    c. the concordance rate for female homosexuality in monozygotic twins is higher than the concordance
       rate for male homosexuality.
    d. a gene exists on the X chromosome that plays a role in the development of sexual orientation.

19. Studies have indicated that female sexual orientation is:

    a. dependent upon genetic factors.
    b. heavily influenced by perinatal exposure to testosterone.
    c. weakly influenced by perinatal exposure to testosterone.
    d. not influenced by ovariectomy.

20. LeVay's study on the role of INAH 3 in sexual orientation should be interpreted with caution because:

    a. it has not yet been replicated.
    b. some unknown 3rd factor may be responsible for both sexual orientation and the size of INAH 3.
    c. LeVay's study was done in gerbils.
    d. it is only a correlational study.

**B. Modified True-False and Fill-in-the Blank Section.** If the statement is true, write TRUE in the blank provided. If the statement is false, write FALSE as well as the word or words that will make the statement true if they replaced the highlighted word or words in the original statement. If the statement is incomplete, write the word or words that will complete it.

1.  **True or False:** Because steroid hormones are synthesized from fat, they **cannot penetrate** a cell's membrane to influence its function.

    **A:** _____

2.  A sperm and an ovum combine to form a _____.

3.  Name the three major classes of gonadal hormones, and give one example of each.

    a._____; e.g., _____

    b._____; e.g., _____

    c._____; e.g., _____

4.  The following sex steroids are released by the testes but not by the ovaries and adrenal cortex:

    _____.

5.  The sex hormones released by the anterior pituitary are referred to as _____.

6.  The pituitary dangles from the _____, on the end of the pituitary stalk.

7.  The two hormones released by the posterior pituitary are _____.

8.  The hypothalamic nuclei that contain the cell bodies of neurons that manufacture the hormones of the posterior pituitary are the _____ nuclei and the _____ nuclei.

9.  **True or False:** Any vein that connects one capillary network with another is called a **portal** vein.

    **A:** _____

10. The only line of communication between the hypothalamus and the anterior pituitary is the _____ system.

11. The first releasing hormone to be isolated was _____ hormone.

12. Virtually all hormones are released from endocrine glands in _____.

13. _____ causes the medulla of each primordial gonad to develop into a testis.

14. At 6 weeks, each human fetus has two sets of reproductive ducts: a female _____ system and a male _____ system.

15. _____ substance causes the Müllerian system to degenerate and the testes to descend into the scrotum.

Chapter 11

16. Female reproductive ducts develop due to a lack of _____ during the critical period of fetal development.

17. **True or False:** Gonadectomy is the same thing as **orchidectomy.**

        **A:** _____

18. During development of the external reproductive organs the labioscrotal swellings grow into the

_____ in males and the labia majora in females.

19. **True or False:** A neonatal female rat was ovariectomized. As an adult, its pattern of gonadotropin release was **cyclic.**

        **A:** _____

20. The _____ nuclei of the preoptic area are larger in male rats and humans than in female rats and humans.

21. All gonadal and adrenal sex hormones are _____ compounds that are synthesized from cholesterol.

22. It has been hypothesized that the conversion of testosterone to _____ is critical for testosterone to masculinize the brain.

23. **True or False:** The aromatization hypothesis of testosterone's effects on the brain is the finding that **dihydrotestosterone** has no masculinizing effect on the rat brain.

        **A:** _____

24. The androgen _____ stimulates the growth of pubic and axillary hair in pubertal females.

25. Many female babies suffering from _____ syndrome are born with an enlarged clitoris and partially fused labia.

26. The key hormones in maintaining the sex drive of human females are thought to be _____.

27. The following are side effects of anabolic steroid abuse. Which are more of a problem for males, and which are more of a problem for females?

    a.    hirsutism:      females ___      males ___

    b.    gynecomastia:      females ___      males ___

    c.    amenorrhea:      females ___      males ___

28. **True or False:** The areas of the hypothalamus that are involved in male and female sexual behavior are the **medial preoptic area and ventromedial hypothalamus**, respectively.

        **A:** _____

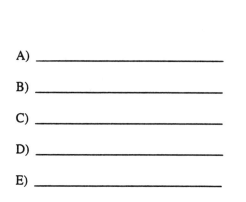

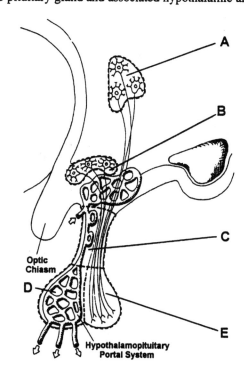

## C. Diagrams.

Figure 1. Identify the following diencephalic and brainstem structures that are involved in the sexual behavior of males and females.

A) _____

B) _____

C) _____

D) _____

E) _____

F) _____

Figure 2. Identify the following structures parts of the pituitary gland and associated hypothalamic areas.

A) _____

B) _____

C) _____

D) _____

E) _____

**D. Short Answer Section.** In no more than 5 sentences, answer each of the following questions.

1. List the three major categories of hormones; include the synthetic precursor for each major category.

2. How does the differentiation of the external reproductive organs differ from the differentiation of the gonads and the internal reproductive ducts?

3. Describe the seminal work of Phoenix and colleagues, who studied the effects of perinatal testosterone on adult copulatory behavior in females and males.

4. Describe the physiological basis for adrenogenital syndrome?  What is the common course of treatment?  What are the problems facing an individual suffering from an untreated case of adrenogenital syndrome?

5. Describe the effects of adult orchidectomy on a person's body and behavior.

6. With respect to the hormonal control of reproductive behavior, how do women differ from the females of other mammalian species?

**Mark your answers to the practice examination; the correct answers follow.  On the basis of your performance, plan the final stages of your studying.**

## Answers to Practice Examination

### A. Multiple Choice Section

| | | | |
|---|---|---|---|
| 1. a; d | 6. a | 11. a | 16. a |
| 2. c | 7. a | 12. b | 17. a |
| 3. a; b; c; d | 8. c | 13. a, b, c, d | 18. a, d |
| 4. b, d | 9. b, c | 14. b, c, d | 19. a, c, d |
| 5. a | 10. b; c; d | 15. b | 20. a, b, d |

### B. Modified True/False and Fill-in-the-Blank Section

1. False; readily penetrate
2. zygote
3. a. androgens; testosterone
   b. estrogens; estradiol
   c. progestins; progesterone
4. There aren't any!
5. gonadotropins
6. hypothalamus
7. vasopressin and oxytocin
8. paraventricular and supraoptic nuclei
9. True
10. hypothalamopituitary portal
11. thyrotropin-releasing
12. pulses
13. H-Y antigen
14. Müllerian; Wolffian
15. Müllerian inhibiting
16. testosterone
17. False; castration
18. scrotum
19. True
20. sexually dimorphic
21. steroid
22. estradiol
23. True
24. androstenedione
25. adrenogenital
26. androgens
27. a) females
    b) males
    c) females
28. True

### C. Diagrams

**Figure 1.** A) Medial Preoptic Area   B) Sexually Dimorphic Nucleus   C) Ventromedial Nucleus
D) Periaqueductal Gray   E) Lateral Tegmental Field   F) Pituitary Gland

**Figure 2.** A) Paraventricular Nucleus   B) Supraoptic Nucleus   C) Pituitary Stalk
D) Anterior Pituitary   E) Posterior Pituitary

### D. Short Answer Section

1. Mention: (1) amino acid derivative hormones synthesized from amino acids (e.g., epinephrine); (2) peptide and protein hormones comprised of chains of amino acids; and (3) steroid hormones synthesized from cholesterol (e.g., androgens and estrogens).

2. In the case of external reproductive organs mention bipotentiality and the role of testosterone; in the case of the gonads and internal ducts mention the female Müllerian system, male Wolffian system, H-Y antigen, testosterone, and Müllerian-inhibiting substance.

3. Mention that these researchers found that perinatal testosterone exposure masculinized and defeminized a genetic females adult copulatory behavior; conversely, perinatal absence of testosterone feminized and demasculinized the adult copulatory behavior of male guinea pigs.

4. Mention it is due to insufficient cortisol secretion, resulting in compensatory adrenal hyperactivity; that it is treated by surgical correction of external genitalia and cortisol administration; that problems stem from the fact that you cannot tell whether the adrenogenital female will be feminized or masculinized at puberty.

5. Mention reduced body hair, fat on the hips and chest, softening of the skin, reduced strength, impotence, sterility.

6. Mention that human female reproductive behavior is not under the control of gonadal hormones; ovariectomy and hormone replacement injections have no effect on it; instead, it is under the control of androgens.

---

# Chapter 12

## SLEEPING, DREAMING, AND CIRCADIAN RHYTHMS

---

## I.  Jeopardy Study Items

*With reference to Chapter 12 of BIOPSYCHOLOGY, write the correct answer to each of the following questions and the correct question for each of the following answers.*

1. What does the case of Miss M. suggest?



2.                                              A:  These are called REMs or rapid eye movements.



3.                                              A:  These measures include the EEG, the EMG, and the EOG.



4. What is the first-night phenomenon?



5.                                              A:  These are called alpha waves.



6.  How does Stage 2 EEG differ from Stage 1?

7. What are the largest and slowest of the normal EEG
   waves called?

8.                                    A: This sleep stage is dominated by delta waves.

9. What is the difference between initial stage 1 and
   emergent stage 1?

10.                                   A: This is also called paradoxical sleep.

11. What term refers to both stage 3 and stage 4 sleep?

12. Sleep is commonly divided into two major categories.
    What are these two categories?

13. What are the physiological correlates of human REM
    sleep?

14. What is the strongest evidence that dreams occur during
    REM sleep?

15.                                   A: This is also called somnambulism.

16                                    A: Despite what some people say, these do not occur during
                                      REM sleep; instead, they usually occur during stage 4 sleep.

Chapter 12

17. Describe the activation-synthesis hypothesis of dream function.

18. What are lucid dreams?

19. What are the recuperative and circadian theories of sleep?

20.                                        A: These are called circadian rhythms.

21.                                        A: These are animals that sleep during the day and are active at night.

22. What is a zeitgeber?

23.                                        A: These are called free-running rhythms.

24. What are three important fundamental properties of free-running periods?

25. What is the evidence that animals can display free-running circadian rhythms without ever experiencing circadian zeitgebers?

26. What does the negative correlation between the duration of a person's sleep and the duration of the preceding period of wakefulness suggest?

27. Describe the phenomenon of internal desynchronization.

28.                                    A: When might you experience phase advances and phase delays, respectively?

29. What can be done to reduce the disruptive effects of shift work and jet lag?

30. What sorts of activities are most disrupted by sleep deprivation?

31. What is the relationship between the duration of sleep deprivation and the magnitude of any performance deficits one might experience?

32.                                    A: These are called microsleeps.

33. What happens when laboratory animals are sleep deprived using the carousel apparatus? Why should these results be interpreted with caution?

34. What are the two major effects of REM-sleep deprivation?

35.                                    A: These are antidepressants that selectively block REM sleep.

36. In what 2 ways does a sleep-deprived person become more "sleep-efficient"?

37. What evidence supports the view that sleep's recuperative function is served specifically by stage 3 and stage 4 sleep?

38.                                            A: This is a cut made between the inferior and the superior colliculi.

39. What effect does the cerveau isolé preparation have on cortical EEG?

40. What is the encéphale isolé preparation, and how does it seem to affect sleep?

41. What is the key difference between Bremer's sensory theory of sleep regulation and the reticular activating system theory?

42. What three early findings supported the reticular-activating theory of sleep?

43.                                            A: These facts suggest that sleep is not a state of neural quiescence.

44. What evidence suggests that there is a sleep-promoting circuit in the caudal brain stem?

45. What evidence suggests that various sleep-stage
correlates of sleep are dissociable?

46.                                           A: These are a cluster of serotonin-producing nuclei running
in a thin strip down the center of the caudal reticular
formation.

47. What effect does serotonin depletion (by PCPA) have on
sleep in most animals?

48. What effect do lesions of the basal forebrain region have
on sleep?

49. What part of the brain seems to play a key role in the
control of REM sleep?

50.                                           A: These neurons coordinate the activity of the REM-sleep
centers in the brainstem.

51.                                           A: These neurons seem to inhibit REM sleep.

52. What evidence suggests that the SCN contains an
important circadian timing mechanism?

53. How did Ralph et al. (1990) use neurotransplantation
procedures to study the SCN?

54.                                         A:  This gene shortens the free-running circadian rhythms of hamsters.

55.  What effect does the gene *clock* have on circadian rhythms?

56.                                         A:  These are the retinohypothalamic tracts.

57.                                         A:  These sleep-altering drugs were originally developed for the treatment of anxiety.

58.  What is 5-HTP?

59.  What kind of sleep is preferentially affected by antihypnotics?

60.  Why is stimulant-drug therapy a risky proposition?

61.                                         A:  This hormone is called  melatonin.

62.  Where is melatonin synthesized in the CNS?

63.  What are the behavioral functions of the pineal gland?

64.  Is the pineal gland critical to the maintenance of circadian rhythms in mammals?

65. Describe the role of melatonin in the generation of sleep.

66. Sleep disorders fall into two complementary categories. What are they?

67. Why do some people complain of sleep disorders when their sleep is normal?

68.                                    A: This is often an iatorgenic sleep disorder.

69. How can tolerance and withdrawal symptoms contribute to the development of insomnia?

70. What is sleep apnea?

71.                                    A: This is called nocturnal myoclonus.

72. How do restless legs produce insomnia?

73. What was the concept of pseudoinsomnia? Why was it abandoned?

74.                           A: This is called narcolepsy.

75.                           A: This is characterized by a sudden loss of muscle tone with no loss of consciousness; a common symptom of narcolepsy

76. Identify the area in the brainstem that seems to be dysfunctional during cataplectic attacks.

77.                           A: This is called a hypnagogic hallucination.

78. What is the only behavioral problem that seems to emerge when someone is limited to less than 6 hr of sleep per night?

79. What is polyphasic sleep?

80. What is sleep inertia?

> **Once you have completed the jeopardy study items, study them. Practice bidirectional studying; make sure that you know the correct answer to every question and the correct question for every answer.**

## II.    Essay Study Questions

*Using Chapter 12 of BIOPSYCHOLOGY, write an outline of the answer to each of the following essay study questions.*

1.  Describe the five stages of sleep EEG and their relation to EMG and EOG changes.

2. Chronologically describe the events of a typical undisturbed night's sleep.

3.  List five common beliefs about sleep and dreaming and what REM-sleep research has revealed about them.

4.  Compare and contrast the recuperative and circadian theories of sleep. Is either one of these theories correct? Justify your answer.

5.  Discuss the factors that play a role in the mammalian circadian sleep-wake cycle. Include information about the SCN and the role of melatonin.

6.  Describe the role of brainstem acetylcholine, norepinephrine, and serotonin neurons in the generation of REM sleep. Which group of transmitters might have their function altered by antidepressant drugs, resulting in the inhibition of REM sleep?

7. Describe the early experiments on the cerveau isolé and the encéphale isolé preparations. What theory of sleep did they suggest?

8. Describe findings that have implicated the suprachiasmatic nuclei and the retinohypothalamic tracts in the establishment of circadian sleep-wake cycles.

9. Describe and briefly discuss four different causes of insomnia: sleeping pills, sleep apnea, myoclonus, and restless legs.

When you have answered the essay study questions, memorize your outlines to prepare for your upcoming examination.

## III.    Practice Examination

*After completing most of your studying of Chapter 12, but at least 24 hours before your formal examination, write the following practice examination.*

**A. Multiple-Choice Section.** Circle the correct answer for each question; *REMEMBER that some questions may have more than one correct answer.*

1. K complexes and sleep spindles are characteristic of:

    a. stage 1 sleep.
    b. stage 2 sleep.
    c. stage 3 sleep.
    d. stage 4 sleep.

2. Delta waves occur during:

    a. stage 1 sleep.
    b. stage 2 sleep.
    c. stage 3 sleep.
    d. stage 4 sleep.

3. REMs typically occur during:

    a. stage 1 sleep EEG.
    b. emergent stage 1 sleep EEG.
    c. initial stage 1 sleep EEG.
    d. stage 4 sleep EEG.

4. It is possible to shorten or lengthen circadian cycles by adjusting:

    a. the free-running period.
    b. the duration of the light-dark cycle.
    c. zeitgebers.
    d. physical exertion.

5. The free-running circadian clock:

    a. is always fast.
    b. is always slow.
    c. is always right on time.
    d. tends to be slow.

6. The simultaneous existence of two different free-running periods in one organism:

    a. suggests that there may be more than one circadian timing mechanism.
    b. is called internal desynchronization.
    c. can be observed in subjects housed in constant environmental conditions.
    d. is not physically possible.

7. Research on polyphasic sleep cycles suggests that:

    a. we have multiple zeitgebers.
    b. naps may have recuperative powers out of proportion to their brevity.
    c. we can do very well if we get at least 6 hr of sleep each night.
    d. naps must be short to avoid sleep inertia.

8. Which of the following research findings supports the idea that it is delta sleep, rather than sleep in general, that serves a recuperative function?

    a. Sleep deprived subjects regain almost all of their lost stage 4 sleep.
    b. Subjects who reduce their sleep times do so by reducing the amount of stage 3 and 4 sleep.
    c. Short sleepers get as much stage 3 and stage 4 sleep as long sleepers.
    d. Extra morning naps contain almost no stage 3 or stage 4 sleep, and they don't reduce the duration of the next night's sleep.

9. The current clinical hypnotics of choice are

    a. tricyclic antidepressants.
    b. stimulants.
    c. benzodiazepines.
    d. barbiturates.

10. Which of the following are sleep disorders?

    a. sleep apnea
    b. sleep paralysis
    c. monophasic sleep cycles
    d. narcolepsy

11. Emergent stage 1 sleep is:

    a. also called REM sleep.
    b. also called paradoxical sleep.
    c. where sleep spindles are seen for the first time in the sleep EEG.
    d. where dreaming most often occurs.

12. The key differences between a cerveau isolé preparation and an encéphale isolé preparation include:

    a. the cerveau isolé preparation involves transection of a very caudal portion of the brainstem.
    b. the cerveau isolé preparation involves transection of a rostral portion of the brainstem.
    c. the cerveau isolé preparation completely eliminates slow-wave sleep.
    d. the cerveau isolé preparation leads to an EEG dominated by short-wave sleep.

**B. Modified True-False and Fill-in-the Blank Section.** If the statement is true, write TRUE in the blank provided. If the statement is false, write FALSE as well as the word or words that will make the statement true if they replaced the highlighted word or words in the original statement. If the statement is incomplete, write the word or words that will complete it.

1. The three standard psychophysiological indices of the stages of sleep are the EEG, the EMG, and the

    _____.

2. All periods of stage 1 sleep EEG other than initial stage 1 sleep EEG are called _____ stage 1 sleep EEG.

3. Stages 2, 3, and 4 are together referred to as _____ sleep.

4. **True or False:** External stimuli presented to a dreaming subject are **never** incorporated into the dream?

    **A:** _____

5. **True or False:** Dreams run on "**real time**", rather than occurring in an instant.

    **A:** _____

6. According to the _____ hypothesis of dreams, the information supplied

    to the cortex during _____ sleep is random; dreams is the cortex's effort to

    make sense of these random signals.

7. **True or False:** Serotonin depletion due to daily PCPA injections only affect sleep in **laboratory rats.**

    **A:** _____

8. **True or False:** Somnambulism is most likely to occur during **dreaming**.

    **A:** _____

9. Circadian rhythms in a constant environment are called _____ rhythms;

    their duration is called the _____ period.

10. Circadian rhythms are entrained by circadian environmental stimuli called _____.

11. Even under free-running conditions, longer periods of wakefulness tend to be followed by

    _____ periods of sleep.

12. It is usually more difficult to adapt to phase _____ than to phase _____.

13. It is usually more difficult to adapt to _____ flights than to _____ flights of the same duration and distance.

14. _____ are brief periods during which the eyelids droop and the sleep-deprived subject becomes unresponsive to external stimuli without losing the ability to sit or stand.

15. Sleep-deprived subjects display deficits on _____ tasks that require continuous attentiveness.

16. The effects of long-term sleep deprivation have been studied in rats using the _____ apparatus.

17. The results of most sleep-deprivation studies are confounded by _____ and _____ disruptions.

18. **True or False: Benzodiazepines** selectively block REM sleep at commonly prescribed clinical doses.

    **A:** _____

19. The two-process model of sleep integrates the effects of both _____ sleep-promoting factors and deprivation-induced sleep-promoting factors.

20. Write either "cerveau" or "encéphale," which ever is more relevant, next to each of the following four phrases.

    a) intracollicular section: _____ isolé

    b) almost continuous high-amplitude, slow-wave EEG: _____ isolé

    c) alternating periods of wakefulness and sleep EEG: _____ isolé

    d) transection of the caudal brain stem: _____ isolé

21. According to the first major active theory of sleep, sleep resulted from low levels of activity in the so-called _____ system.

22. It has been hypothesized that there are sleep-promoting circuits in the serotonergic _____ nuclei, in other nuclei of the caudal brain stem, and in the basal _____ region.

23. The major circadian timing mechanism appears to be in the _____ nuclei.

24. Visual zeitgebers entrain circadian rhythms through signals carried by the _____ tracts.

25. Research on the mechanisms of cataplexy have linked it to _____ sleep and the cells of the _____.

26. **True or False:** Insomnia that is caused by prescribed sleeping pills is said to be **iatrogenic**.

    **A:** _____

27. _____ is frequently caused by the withdrawal effect of most sleep-promoting drugs.

28. People who take sleeping pills typically become _____ to their soporific (sleep-promoting) effects, and thus they take larger and larger doses of them.

29. In some cases of sleep _____, spasms of the throat muscles block the intake of air.

Chapter 12

## C. Diagrams

Figure 1.  Identify the 6 brain regions involved in sleep that are illustrated below.

A) _____

B) _____

C) _____

D) _____

E) _____

F) _____

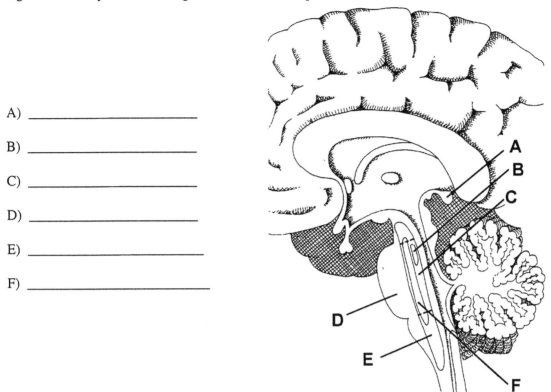

**D. Short Answer Section.**  In no more than 5 sentences, answer each of the following questions.

1. Describe the two theories that account for why we sleep.  How does Borbély (1984) deal with the existence of two theories?

2. Describe what is known about genetic regulation of circadian rhythms.

3. Describe the experiments that led to the discovery of the retinohypothalamic tracts.

4. Describe the three most important findings about the neural basis of sleep that followed the discovery of the reticular activating system.

Mark your answers to the practice examination; the correct answers follow. On the basis of your performance, plan the final stages of your studying.

## Answers to Practice Examination

### A. Multiple Choice Section

1. b
2. c, d
3. b
4. b, c, d
5. d
6. a, b, c

7. b, d
8. a, c, d
9. c
10. a, d
11. a, b, d
12. b, d

### B. Modified True/False and Fill-in-the-Blank Section

1. EOG
2. emergent
3. slow-wave
4. False; often
5. True
6. activation-synthesis hypothesis
7. False; cats
8. False; stage 4
9. free-running; free-running
10 zeitgebers
11. shorter
12. advances; delays
13. eastern; western
14. Microsleeps
15. boring (or equivalent)
16. carousel
17. stress; circadian

18. False; tricyclic antidepressants
19. circadian
20. a) cerveau
    b) cerveau
    c) encéphale
    d) encéphale
21. reticular activating
22. raphé; forebrain
23. suprachiasmatic
24. retinohypothalamic
25. REM; nucleus magnocellularis
26. True
27. insomnia
28. tolerant
29. apnea

### C. Diagrams

Figure 1. A) Pineal Gland   B) Locus Coeruleus   C) Pontine Reticular Formation   D) Pons
E)  Medullary Reticular Formation   F) Raphé Nucleus

### D. Short Answer Section

1. Mention the recuperation theories (sleep restores some homeostatic imbalance) and the circadian theories (sleep makes us inactive when we do not need to be active); the synthesis of circadian and recuperative sleep-promoting factors in the integrated theory of Borbély.

2. Mention the genes *tau* and *clock*; the shortening of circadian rhythm in hamsters with *tau;* the absence of intrinsic circadian rhythms in mice carrying the *clock* mutation.

3. Mention the retinothalamic pathway (optic nerves, optic chiasm, optic tracts to lateral geniculate of thalamus); the disruption in circadian rhythm produced by cuts placed before, but not after, the optic chiasm; the discovery of the retinohypothalamic pathway to the SCN *before* the optic chiasm.

4. Mention that sleep is not a state of neural quiescence; that there are several different sleep-promoting circuits in the brain; that the various correlates of sleep (e.g., REM; SWS) can be dissociated.

# Chapter 13

# DRUG ABUSE AND REWARD CIRCUITS IN THE BRAIN

## I.    Jeopardy Study Items

*With reference to Chapter 13 of BIOPSYCHOLOGY, write the correct answer to each of the following questions and the correct question for each of the following answers.*

1. Approximately how many people are addicted to illicit
   drugs in the United States?


2.                                                    A:  This is called a psychoactive drug.


3.                                                    A: These routes of administration include ingestion,
                                                      injection, inhalation, or absorption through mucous
                                                      membranes.


4. Identify 3 common methods of drug injection.


5. Which route of drug administration is preferred by many
   chronic drug addicts?  Why?


6. What makes it difficult for many drugs to pass from the
   circulatory system into the CNS?

Chapter 13

7. Identify at least 3 mechanisms of drug action.

8. What is drug metabolism? Why is it an important determinant of drug action?

9.                                          A: This is called drug tolerance.

10. In what two ways can drug tolerance be demonstrated?

11.                                         A: This is called sensitization.

12. What is metabolic tolerance?

13. What is functional tolerance?

14.                                         A: This is called a drug withdrawal syndrome.

15.                                         A: These people are said to be physically dependent upon a drug's effects.

16. What is the difference between addiction, physical dependence, and psychological dependence?

17. What is contingent drug tolerance?

18.                                              A: This research design is used in most demonstrations of contingent drug tolerance.

19.                                              A: This is called conditioned drug tolerance.

20. What does the phrase "situational specificity of drug tolerance" refer to?

21. What is a conditioned compensatory response?

22.                                              A: This is called a conditioned withdrawal effect.

23.                                              A: This is the second most frequently used drug in the world.

24. Is nicotine addictive? Justify your answer.

25. What are the long-term consequences of smoking tobacco?

26. What is Buerger's disease, and what point does it make about the addiction potential of tobacco?

27. What are free radicals? How might they play a role in nicotine's pathological effects?

28. Is ethanol a stimulant or a depressant? Justify your answer.

29.                                    A: This is euphemistically referred to as a hangover.

30. What are the symptoms of the alcohol withdrawal syndrome?

31.                                    A: These include Korsakoff's syndrome, cirrhosis of the liver, heart attack, and gastritis.

32.                                    A: This is called fetal alcohol syndrome.

33. What is delta-9-THC?

34. Describe the effects of low doses of marijuana.

35. What are the hazards of long-term marijuana use?

36.                                    A: This is generally referred to as the marijuana amotivational syndrome.

37. What are some of clinically beneficial effects of THC?

38. What is a stimulant?

39. Describe the behavioral effects of cocaine.

40.                                        A:  This is called a cocaine spree.

41.                                        A:  These include amphetamine, methamphetamine, and MDMA.

42. What is the relation between opium, morphine, codeine, and heroin?

43.                                        A:  These clinically useful effects include analgesia, cough suppression, and the treatment of diarrhea.

44. What is the Harrison Narcotic Act?  How did it increase heroin addiction?

45. What are the <u>direct</u> health hazards of opiate addiction?

Chapter 13

46. Opiate withdrawal is one of the most misunderstood
    aspects of drug use.  Why?



47.                                     A:  These include poverty, poor medical care, poor diet,
                                        arrest, AIDS, and death from overdose.


48.  What are endorphins?



49.  Describe the physical-dependence theory of addiction.




50.  What are two problems with the theory that conditioned
     withdrawal effects motivate relapse?



51.                                     A:  These people are called *needle freaks*.



52.  Describe the positive-incentive theory of drug addiction.




53.  Describe the role of drug-induced sensitization in
     Robinson and Berridge's incentive-sensitization theory
     of drug abuse.




54.  Why is the phenomenon of intracranial self-stimulation
     interesting to those searching for the neural basis of
     addiction?

55.                                        A: This is called priming.

56.                                        A: This is called the mesotelencephalic dopamine system.

57. Describe the evidence that mesotelencephalic dopamine
    plays a key role in ICSS and other reward phenomena.

58. What is 6-hydroxydopamine? How is it used to study
    the neural bases of addiction and reinforcement?

59. What are consummatory behaviors and preparatory
    behaviors?

60. What is the conditioned-place-preference paradigm?
    What is its main advantage?

> **Once you have completed the jeopardy study items, study them. Practice bidirectional studying; make sure that you know the correct answer to every question and the correct question for every answer.**

Chapter 13

## II. Essay Study Questions

*Using Chapter 13 of BIOPSYCHOLOGY, write an outline of the answer to each of the following essay study questions.*

1. What is drug tolerance? Describe at least 2 ways that drug tolerance influences drug consumption.

2. "Drug tolerance effects and drug withdrawal effects are commonly assumed to be different manifestations of the same physiological changes". What does this mean?

3. Compare and contrast the phenomena of contingent drug tolerance and conditioned drug tolerance. Provide an example of each kind of tolerance.

4. Compare and contrast the various methods of drug administration. Why would intracranial administration of a drug be so effective; provide at least 2 plausible reasons.

5. Discuss the direct health hazards of tobacco, alcohol, marijuana, cocaine, and heroin. On the basis of this discussion, rank them in order of dangerousness to the drug taker.

6. Discuss common misconceptions about drug abuse and about the best way to deal with the drug-abuse problem. Then discuss some of the "expert opinions" offered as solutions to the drug problem.

Chapter 13

7.  Compare the physical-dependence theory of addiction with the positive-incentive theory of addiction.

8.  Describe the main features of the intracranial self-stimulation phenomenon.

9.  Describe the mesotelencephalic dopamine pathways and the evidence suggesting that they play a key role in reward and reinforcement.

---

**When you have answered the essay study questions, memorize your outlines to prepare for your upcoming examination.**

## III.  Practice Examination

*After completing most of your studying of Chapter 13, but at least 24 hours before your formal examination, write the following practice examination.*

**A. Multiple-Choice Section.**  Circle the correct answer for each question; *REMEMBER that some questions may have more than one correct answer.*

1. A major disadvantage of the oral route of drug administration relative to other routes is its:

    a. unpredictability.
    b. safety.
    c. rapid onset of effectiveness.
    d. long-term effectiveness.

2. The actions of most drugs on the central nervous system are terminated by:

    a. elimination.
    b. metabolism.
    c. diffusion.
    d. the blood brain barrier.

3. Functional tolerance is due to:

    a. a decrease in the amount of drug getting to its sites of action
    b. a shift in the dose-response curve to the left.
    c. a decrease in reactivity of the sites of action to the drug.
    d. increased metabolism of the drug.

4. Withdrawal syndromes:

    a. indicate a state of physical dependency on the drug.
    b. vary in severity depending on the drug.
    c. vary in severity depending on the speed of drug elimination.
    d. are typically characterized by effects that are opposite to those of the drug.

5. The before-and-after design is used to study:

    a. metabolic tolerance.
    b. contingent tolerance.
    c. conditioned tolerance.
    d. situation-specific tolerance.

6. According to Ramsay and Woods, the unconditional stimulus in a drug-taking situation is:

    a. the environment that the drug is consumed in.
    b. the drug that is consumed.
    c. the effects of the drug on the organism's physiology.
    d. the response of the organism to the drug's effects.

7. There is some suggestion that many tobacco-related disorders occur as a result of the presence of _____ in tobacco.

    a. nicotine
    b. tar
    c. free radicals
    d. solvents

8. Chronic exposure to alcohol can produce:

    a. functional tolerance.
    b. metabolic tolerance.
    c. brain damage.
    d. physical dependence.

9. Korsakoff's syndrome is a neuropathological disorder that is:

    a. characterized by seizures and a loss of consciousness.
    b. characterized by severe memory loss.
    c. caused by excessive, prolonged ethanol consumption.
    d. caused by cirrhosis of the liver.

10. One of the difficulties in characterizing the effects of marijuana is that:

    a. a pure form of the active ingredient is not available.
    b. the active ingredient does not bind to a specific receptor in the brain.
    c. they are subtle
    d. they are greatly influenced by social situation

11. Cocaine exerts its behavioral effects by:

    a. interacting with catecholamine receptors.
    b. increasing reuptake of catecholamines.
    c. decreasing reuptake of catecholamines.
    d. increasing the synthesis of catecholamines.

12. Psychostimulant drugs that have been shown to produce bran damage include:

    a) methamphetamine.
    b) cocaine
    c) caffeine
    d) MDMA

13. Opiates are extremely effective in the treatment of:

    a. pain
    b. cough
    c. diarrhea
    d. glaucoma

14. Evidence against the physical-dependence theory of addiction includes the observation that:

    a. detoxified addicts often return to former drug-taking habits.
    b. highly addictive drugs, such as alcohol, produce severe withdrawal distress.
    c. highly addictive drugs, such as cocaine, do not produce severe withdrawal distress.
    d. the pattern of drug taking displayed by many addicts involves periods of detoxification.

15. Early research led to the theory that reinforcement is mediated by activation of the:

    a. septum.
    b. fornix.
    c. mesotelencephalic dopamine system.
    d. lateral hypothalamus.

16. In one well known experiment, unilateral injections of 6-OHDA into the mesotelencephalic dopamine system:

    a. increased self-stimulation from ipsilateral brain sites.
    b. increased self-stimulation from contralateral brain sites.
    c. decreased self-stimulation from contralateral brain sites.
    d. decreased self-stimulation from ipsilateral sites.

17. Two of the following lines of evidence suggest that the rewarding effects of opiates are mediated by the mesotelencephalic dopamine system. Which two?

    a. Rats lever press for microinjections of opiates into the ventral tegmental area or nucleus accumbens.
    b. Dopamine antagonists block the conditioned place preference normally produced by opiates.
    c. Dopamine agonists block the conditioned place preference normally produced by opiates.
    d. Rats lever press for electrical stimulation of the mesotelencephalic dopamine system.

18. Which of the following has been shown to block the rewarding effects of intravenous stimulants in experiments on laboratory animals?

    a. lesions of the nucleus accumbens or ventral tegmental area
    b. norepinephrine antagonists
    c. norepinephrine agonists
    d. dopamine agonists

19. Freud's famous "Song of Praise" was:

    a. about the value of cocaine in psychotherapy.
    b. about his love of cigars.
    c. criticized by many of his peers.
    d. about his battle with cancer.

20. In general, government policy towards problems with drug abuse and addiction have been:

    a. very effective at curbing drug use in North America.
    b. governed by the philosophy that drug abuse and addiction are diseases.
    c. governed by the philosophy that drug abuse and addiction are criminal acts.
    d. most beneficial to those who sell illegal drugs.

**B. Modified True-False and Fill-in-the Blank Section.** If the statement is true, write TRUE in the blank provided. If the statement is false, write FALSE as well as the word or words that will make the statement true if they replaced the highlighted word or words in the original statement. If the statement is incomplete, write the word or words that will complete it.

1. What do the following abbreviations stand for?

    a) IM: _____

    b) IV: _____

    c) SC: _____

2. _____ is a common drug of abuse that is usually self-administered through the mucous membranes.

3. **True or False:** Tolerance is a shift in the dose-response curve to the **left**.

    A: _____

4. Individuals who suffer withdrawal reactions when they stop taking a drug are said to be

    _____ on the drug.

5. In one study, tolerance did not develop to the anticonvulsant effect of alcohol unless

    _____ was administered during the periods of alcohol exposure.

6. According to Siegel, _____ responses become conditioned to environments in which drug effects are repeatedly experienced; these responses offset the effects of the drug and proudce tolerance.

7. **True or False:** According to the **positive-incentive** theory of addiction, addicts become trapped in a vicious circle of drug taking and withdrawal symptoms.

    A: _____

8. Which of the following is related to the intracranial self stimulation phenomenon and which is not?

    a) slow extinction             yes ___         no ___

    b) priming                       yes ___         no ___

    c) high response rates         yes ___         no ___

    d) Olds and Milner           yes ___         no ___

9. The theory that ascending dopamine projections play a major role in intracranial self-stimulation is supported by the finding that positive mesencephalic ICSS sites are localized in the

    _____.

10. **True or False:** The incentive value of a drug can be measured in laboratory animals in the **place preference conditioning** paradigm, unconfounded by other effects of the drug on behavior.

 A: _____

11. **True or False:** During his life, the famous psychoanalyst Sigmund Freud became addicted to **nicotine** and to **opium**.

 A: _____

12. Next to each of the following phrases write the name of the relevant drug.

a) major active ingredient of tobacco: _____

b) major active ingredient of opium: _____

c) major active ingredient of marijuana: _____

d) Buerger's disease: _____

e) lung cancer, emphysema: _____

f) glaucoma: _____

g) Korsakoff's syndrome: _____

h) amotivational syndrome: _____

i) alleviates glaucoma and nausea: _____

j) crack: _____

k) diuretic: _____

l) soldier's disease: _____

m) Coca Cola: _____

n) Dalby's Carminative: _____

o) gold turkey and goose flesh: _____

p) sensitization, sprees, psychosis: _____

q) cirrhosis: _____

r) morphine, codeine, heroin: _____

## C. Diagrams

**Figure 1.** Label the following dose-response curve illustrating the phenomenon of drug tolerance.

A) _____

B) _____

C) _____

D) _____

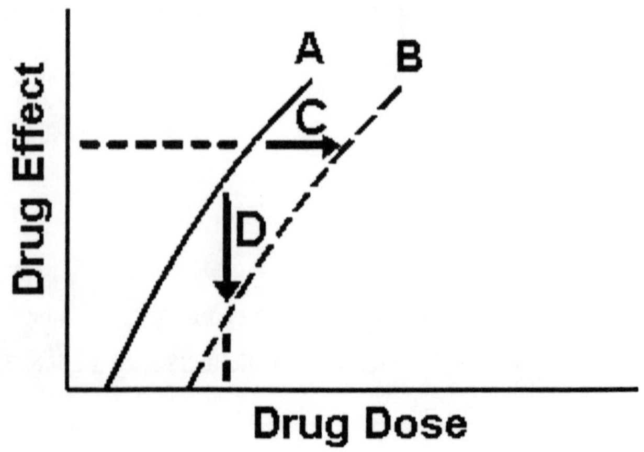

## C. Diagrams, *continued.*

**Figure 2.** Identify these neural structures that comprise key elements of the mesotelencephalic dopamine
pathway.

A) _____     E) _____

B) _____     F) _____

C) _____     G) _____

D) _____     H) _____

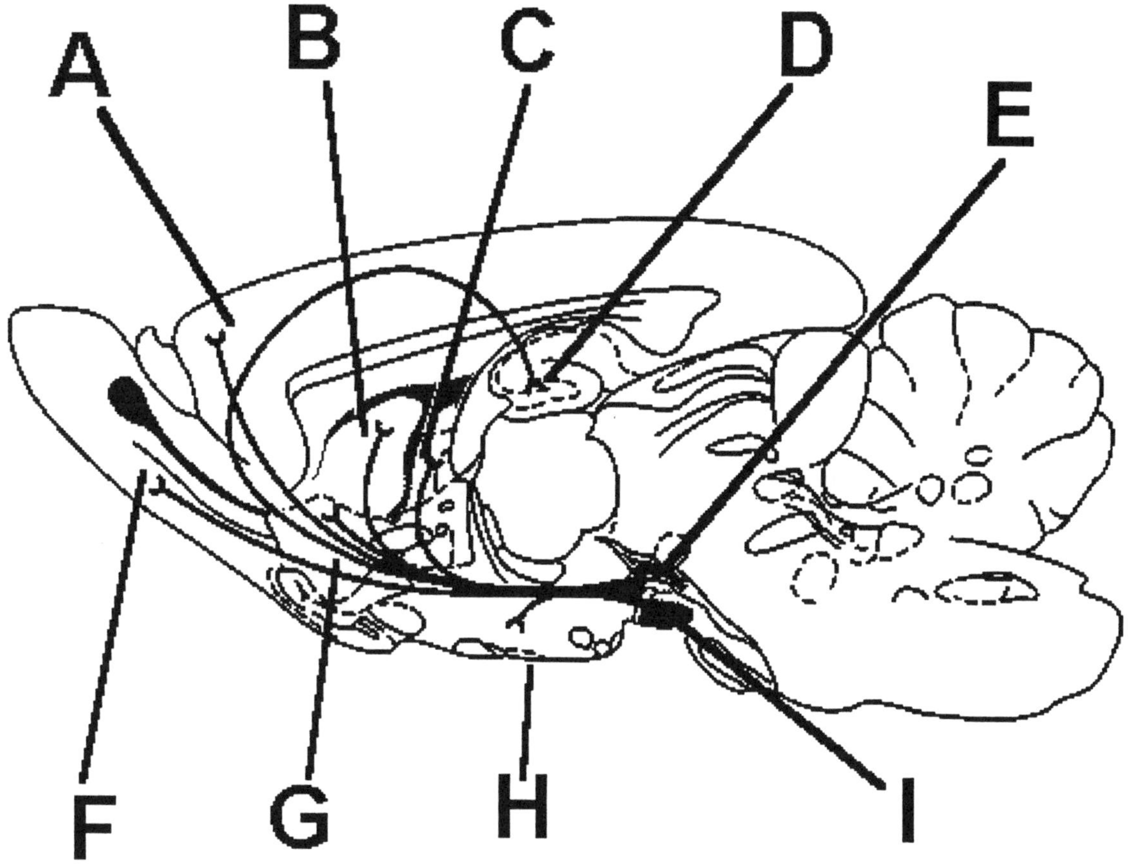

**D. Short Answer Section.** In no more than 5 sentences, answer each of the following questions.

1. Define the term "drug tolerance"; list 3 important points about the specificity of drug tolerance.

2. Describe the relation between addiction, withdrawal and physical dependence.

3. "Many in the scientific community are frustrated with a drug policy that treats addiction as a crime rather than a disease." Discuss the basis for this statement.

4. Describe conditioned drug tolerance and provide one example of tolerance that supports this model.

5. Describe physical-dependence theories of drug addiction. Explain how these theories attempt to account for the fact that addicts frequently relapse even after lengthy drug-free periods.

6. Describe the positive-incentive theory of addiction. Include the factors that are hypothesized to maintain early bouts of drug administration as well as factors that might maintain long-term drug consumption.

7. What is the key neural substrate underlying the phenomenon of intracranial self-stimulation? Describe at least two types of research that support the view that this system of neurons is involved in many different types of reward.

8. What are the two different phases of naturally motivated behaviors? On the basis of current evidence, which of these two phases is now thought to be regulated by the mesotelencephalic dopamine system?

9. Describe the drug self-administration paradigm and the conditioned place-preference paradigm. What is the major advantage of the conditioned place-preference paradigm?

**Mark your answers to the practice examination; the correct answers follow. On the basis of your performance, plan the final stages of your studying.**

# Answers to Practice Examination

## A. Multiple Choice Section

| | | | |
|---|---|---|---|
| 1. a | 6. c | 11. c | 16. d |
| 2. b | 7. c | 12. a, b, d | 17. a, b |
| 3. c | 8. a, b, c, d | 13. a, b, c | 18. a |
| 4. a, b, c, d | 9. b, c | 14. a, c, d | 19. a, c |
| 5. b | 10. c, d | 15. a, d | 20. c, d |

## B. Modified True/False and Fill-in-the-Blank Section

1. a) intramuscular
   b) intravenous
   c) subcutaneous
2. cocaine
3. False: right
4. physically dependent
5. convulsive stimulation (or equivalent)
6. conditioned compensatory
7. False: physical-dependence
8. a) no
   b) yes
   c) yes
   d) yes
9. ventral tegmental area
10. True
11. True

12. a) nicotine
    b) morphine
    c) delta-9-THC
    d) nicotine (or tobacco)
    e) nicotine (or tobacco)
    f) delta-9-THC
    g) alcohol
    h) marijuana (or delta-9-THC)
    i) marijuana (or delta-9-THC)
    j) cocaine
    k) alcohol
    l) morphine
    m) cocaine
    n) opium
    o) heroin (or morphine)
    p) cocaine
    q) alcohol
    r) opiates

## C. Diagrams

**Figure 1.** (see Fig. 13.2)

A) Initial dose-response curve   B) Dose response curve after repeated exposure to drug
C) An increase in drug dose is necessary to maintain the same effect.
D) At the same drug dose, the drug effect is reduced

**Figure 2.** (see Fig. 13.10)

A) Prefrontal Cortex   B) Striatum   C) Septum   D) Hippocampus   E) Ventral Tegmental Area
F) Olfactory Tubercle   G) Nucleus Accumbens   H) Amygdala   I) Substantia Nigra

## D. Short Answer Section

1. Mention that tolerance is a shift in the dose-response curve to the right; that cross tolerance sometimes develops between drug effects; that tolerance develops to some drug effects but not others; that the development of tolerance is not subserved by a single mechanism.

2. Mention that addiction is not related to either withdrawal or physical dependence (e.g., cocaine is very addictive yet elicits few withdrawl or physical dependence symptoms); that the occurrence of withdrawal symptoms indicates physical dependence.

3. Mention that the current drug policies in many countries, which view drug addiction as a crime rather than a disease, have failed to stem the tide of drug abuse; that they have instead resulted in increased crime, increased law enforcement costs, increased medical care, crowded jails, and rich drug dealers.

4. Mention that the drug recipient will be tolerant only when the drug is experienced in an environment that has become associated with its effects; examples could include conditioned tolerance to the hypothermic effects of alcohol or to the lethal effects of opiates.

5. Mention that drug taking is hypothesized to occur to avoid withdrawal symptoms; that these theories postulate that withdrawal symptoms can be elicited by conditional stimuli and as a result addicts may relapse after detoxification when they encounter a drug-predictive environment.

6. Mention that drug taking is hypothesized to initially occur in order to obtain the pleasurable effects of the drug; over time, the positive-incentive value of drugs will increase due to sensitization, increasing desire for the drug out of proportion to any pleasure the drug effects may hold.

7. Mention the mesotelencephalic dopamine system and the ventral tegmental area; list some combination of stimulaltion mapping studies, microdialysis studies, dopamine agonist and antagonist studies, and lesion studies.

8. Mention consummatory behaviors and preparatory behaviors; that the former complete a sequence of motivated behavior (i.e., copulation) whereas the latter enable an organism to perform a consummatory response (i.e., approaching a sex partner); that mesotelencephalic dopamine is thought to play a more important role in preparatory behaviors.

9. Mention that drug self-administration involves animals pressing a lever drug that is administered by an intravenous catheter; that place-preference conditioning involves pairing drug exposure with a specific environment, which animals come to prefer over a control compartment; that place-preference conditioning has the advantage that subjects are tested drug-free, ensuring that the incentive value of the drug is not confounded by its other behavioral effects.

---

# Chapter 14

## MEMORY AND AMNESIA

---

**I.    Jeopardy Study Items**

*With reference to Chapter 14 of BIOPSYCHOLOGY, write the correct answer to each of the following questions and the correct question for each of the following answers.*

1.                                          A:  This refers to the brain's ability to stored the learned effects of its experience.

2.                                          A:  This is called the engram.

3.    Define the principle of mass action and the principle of equipotentiality, respectively.

4.                                          A:  This means "pertaining to memory".

5.    What is memory consolidation?

6.	A:  This is called a reverberatory circuit.

7.	What was the most important prediction made from
	Hebb's theory of memory consolidation?

8.	What is a bilateral medial temporal lobectomy?

9.	What are the two major subcortical structures of the
	medial temporal lobes?

10.	A:  These are called a lobectomy and a lobotomy,
	respectively.

11.	What is the difference between anterograde and
	retrograde amnesia?

12.	Who is H.M.?

13.	What is H.M.'s most devastating memory problem?

14.	Why was H.M. able to perform the verbal matching-to-
	sample task, but not the nonverbal form of the task?

15.	A:  This is called the mirror-drawing task.

16. Describe H.M.'s performance on the following
memory tests; when a description of his performance
is already given, name the test.

   a.  digit span +1 test:

   b.                                          A: His performance on this version of the block-tapping
                                               memory-span test was very poor.

   c.  verbal and nonverbal matching-to-sample tests

   d.                                          A: On each trial, he went outside the boundaries less
                                               frequently, but he had no recollection of previously
                                               performing the task.

   e.  rotary-pursuit task

   f.  incomplete-pictures test

   g.                                          A: H.M. had trouble identifying or explaining ambiguous
                                               sentences.

   h.                                          A: after 2 years, H.M. performed this task almost perfectly

17. How did H.M.'s deficits refute the notion that each part
   of the forebrain participates equivalently in the storage
   of memory?

18.                                            A: This theory was supported by the fact that H.M.'s surgery
                                               abolished the formation of certain kinds of long-term
                                               memories while leaving his short-term memory intact.

19.  What is the difference between explicit (declarative; conscious) memory and implicit (procedural; unconscious) memory?

20.  How long was H.M.'s gradient of retrograde amnesia? What did the length of this gradient suggest about the neural basis of consolidation?

21.  What is "repetition priming"?

22.  Why is patient R.B. so significant to the idea that hippocampal damage produces memory deficits?

23.  What is Korsakoff's syndrome?

24.                                          A: This has been difficult to determine because the brain damage is so diffuse in Korsakoff's patients.

25.  What is the anatomical basis of the memory loss that is observed in patients with Korsakoff's syndrome?

26.  What did an MRI of N.A.'s brain suggest about the neural bases of diencephalic amnesia?

27.  How is memory impaired following damage to the prefrontal cortex?

28.                                          A: These are called self-ordered tasks.

29.                                    A: These include neurofibrils, amyloid plaques, and neural degeneration.

30. What evidence links cholinergic dysfunction to Alzheimer's disease?

31.                                    A: These include the nucleus basalis of Meynert, the diagonal band of Broca, and the medial septal nucleus.

32.                                    A: This is called a nootropic.

33. What is the most common cause of amnesia? What is this kind of amnesia called?

34.                                    A: These are called islands of memory.

35. What is ECS? What is it clinically used for?

36. What did early work in the area of ECS and memory suggest about consolidation?

37. What did Squire and his colleagues demonstrate about retrograde amnesia gradients in human patients after ECS?

38. Why were early attempts to produce an animal model of H.M.'s memory deficits such dismal failures?

39.                                    A: This behavioral paradigm is called the nonrecurring-items delayed nonmatching-to-sample task.

40. What is the Mumby box?

41. What cortical area seems to play a critical role in the amnesiac effects of medial temporal lobe lesions on object recognition?

42. Describe how Mumby and his colleagues convincingly demonstrated that ischemia-induced memory deficits are not due to hippocampal damage.

43. What kinds of memories are most consistently impaired in rats with hippocampal damage?

44.                                          A: These tasks are called the Morris water maze and the radial arm maze.

45. What is the difference between working and reference memory?

46.                                          A: These are called hippocampal place cells.

47. What type of glutamate receptor seems to play a key role in the establishment of hippocampal place fields?

48. What is the cognitive-map theory of hippocampal function?

49. What are two alternatives to the cognitive-map theory of hippocampal function?

50. Describe the role of the amygdala in memory.

51. According to current theories, where are memories stored?

52. Describe the role of the cerebellum in memory for the conditioned eye-blink response.

53.                                        A: This structure stores memories for consistent relationships between stimuli.

54.                                        A: This structure contributes to memories for the specific order of events.

55. Describe the differential role for the left and right anterior prefrontal cortex in the retrieval of declarative memories.

56. What suggests that the dorsomedial nuclei and the medial temporal lobes may be components of the same memory circuit?

57.                                        A: This is called pyrithiamine.

58. Does the basal forebrain have a role in memory?

---

**Once you have completed the jeopardy study items, study them. Practice bidirectional studying; make sure that you know the correct answer to every question and the correct question for every answer.**

## II.    Essay Study Questions

*Using Chapter 14 of BIOPSYCHOLOGY, write an outline of the answer to each of the following essay study questions.*

1.  Describe H.M.'s surgery and summarize the effects that it had on his performance of at least 3 different tests of memory. How did H.M. revolutionize the study of the neural bases of memory?

2.  What six important ideas about the biopsychology of memory are, to a large degree, a legacy of H.M.'s case?

3.  Describe patient N.A. What has he revealed to researchers about the importance of diencephalic structures to the neural bases of memory?

4. Compare and contrast the memory deficits associated with bilateral medial temporal lobectomy and Korsakoff's disease. What might account for these differences?

5. Describe the anterograde and retrograde amnesia observed after a closed-head injury. What does the nature of these disturbances suggest about memory?

6. Describe the nonrecurring-items delayed nonmatching-to-sample task. What has this task revealed about the neural bases of memory?

7.  Compare and contrast the cognitive-mapping theory, the configural learning theory, and the path-integration theory of hippocampal function.

8.  Describe the role of the rhinal cortex in object-recognition memory, citing data from both human and nonhuman primate studies and rodent studies.

9.  Compare the memory deficits observed in patients with Alzheimer's disease with those of patient H.M. and patients suffering from Korsakoff's disease. What might account for these differences?

10. Describe the role of the hippocampus in spatial memory; include evidence from behavioral, electrophysiological, lesions, and genetic studies.

11. The prefrontal cortex is emerging as a key neural structure in memory function. Describe data supporting this idea, including evidence from patients suffering from different forms of neuropathology and from recent imaging studies.

12. Describe the role of the cerebellum and striatum in memory.

When you have answered the essay study questions, memorize your outlines to prepare for your upcoming examination.

## III.   Practice Examination

*After completing most of your studying of Chapter 14, but at least 24 hours before your formal examination, write the following practice examination.*

A. **Multiple-Choice Section.**  Circle the correct answer for each question; *REMEMBER that some questions may have more than one correct answer.*

1.  According to Hebb's two-stage theory of memory storage, short-term memories were stored by:

     a.  consolidation.
     b.  reverberating neural activity.
     c.  long-term memories.
     d.  synaptic disinhibition.

2.  A deficit in the retrieval of information that was learned before an accident represents a case of:

     a.  consolidation.
     b.  ischemia.
     c.  retrograde amnesia.
     d.  explicit memory.

3.  H.M.'s operation involved bilateral removal of:

     a.  the hippocampus.
     b.  the dorsomedial nucleus of the thalamus.
     c.  the amygdala.
     d.  the prefrontal cortex.

4.  In terms of its effect on his epilepsy, H.M.'s bilateral medial temporal lobectomy was:

     a.  a modest failure.
     b.  a modest success.
     c.  an unqualified success.
     d.  a dismal failure.

5.  After his operation, H.M. had:

     a.  a mild retrograde amnesia for the events of the year or two preceding surgery.
     b.  a severe anterograde amnesia.
     c.  a severe retrograde amnesia for remote events (e.g., the events of his childhood).
     d.  a mild anterograde amnesia.

6.  H.M.'s ability to perform tests of short-term memory (e.g., the digit span test) are:

     a.  nonexistent.
     b.  severely disturbed.
     c.  severely disturbed, but only some of the time.
     d.  reasonably normal.

7. Which of the following statements about H.M.'s case is not true? H.M.'s case

    a. was one of the first to implicate the medial temporal lobes in memory.
    b. strongly challenged the view that there are two physiologically distinct modes of storage for short-term and long-term memory.
    c. was among the first clear demonstrations of the survival of implicit long-term memory in an amnesic subject.
    d. showed that gradients of retrograde amnesia could cover very long periods of time.

8. An autopsy revealed that R.B. had ischemia-produced damage to the:

    a. hippocampus.
    b. pyramidal cell layer.
    c. CA1 subfield.
    d. amygdala

9. Evidence suggests that the amnesic symptoms of Korsakoff's syndrome are attributable, at least in part, to damage to:

    a. the dorsomedial nuclei of the thalamus.
    b. the prefrontal cortex.
    c. the hippocampus.
    d. a variety of diencephalic structures.

10. N.A. suffers from a:

    a. large ischemia-produced infarction.
    b. bilateral thalamic lesion.
    c. large lesion of the medial diencephalon.
    d. lesion that is restricted to one dorsomedial nucleus of the thalamus.

11. Evidence suggests that some of the memory deficits of Korsakoff patients are attributable to damage to prefrontal cortex. These memory deficits include their:

    a. failure to release from proactive interference.
    b. inability to form implicit memories.
    c. poor memory for temporal sequence.
    d. deficits on delayed matching-to-sample tasks.

12. In patients with Alzheimer's disease, there is:

    a. a major selective reduction in dopamine.
    b. less choline acetyltransferase.
    c. less acetylcholinesterase.
    d. a major reduction in cholinergic receptors.

13. After his electroconvulsive therapy, Craig did not remember any thing about his week of hospitalization except Carolyn's visit on the third day. This recollection is:

    a. short-term memory.
    b. an island of memory.
    c. an implicit memory.
    d. hypermetaamnesia.

14. In a study that examined amnesia for television shows, Squire and his colleagues found a gradient of retrograde amnesia in patients after electroconvulsive therapy; the gradient covered about:

   a. 1 minute.
   b. 5 minutes.
   c. 1 hour.
   d. 3 years.

15. According to the configural-association theory of hippocampal function, the hippocampus:

   a. is responsible for the memories of individual stimuli.
   b. is responsible for memories of the relationships between stimuli.
   c. is responsible only for spatial memory, such as that required to perform the Morris water maze.
   d. has a role in the formation of all explicit memories.

16. Humans with prefrontal cortex lesions display memory deficits in their:

   a. ability to remember the sequence of events.
   b. ability to remember which tasks they have completed and which tasks have yet to be done.
   c. ability to perform the digit-span test.
   d. ability to perform the delayed-non-matching-to-sample test.

17. Which of the following lies within the boundaries of the medial temporal lobe?

   a. entorhinal cortex
   b. hippocampus
   c. amygdala
   d. mammillary bodies

18. The ability for a blind-folded rat to run back to its home cage, independent of allocentric cues, is an example of:

   a. consolidation.
   b. path integration.
   c. behavior based upon egocentric cues.
   d. anterograde memory.

19. The mnemonic function of the cerebellum is believed to include a role in:

   a. place conditioning.
   b. storage for memories of different sensorimotor skills.
   c. storage for memories about consistent relationships between stimuli and responses.
   d. storage for the order of events.

20. Evidence that the dorsomedial nuclei of the thalamus plays a role in memory includes:

   a. exposure to pyrithiamine produces lesions in the dorsomedial nuclei and a variety of memory deficits.
   b. the results of MRI scans done on patient NA.
   c. the effects of ischemia on mnemonic function.
   d. results of PET studies of the human brain during various tests of memory function.

**B. Modified True-False and Fill-in-the Blank Section.** If the statement is true, write TRUE in the blank provided. If the statement is false, write FALSE as well as the word or words that will make the statement true if they replaced the highlighted word or words in the original statement. If the statement is incomplete, write the word or words that will complete it.

1. **True or False:** The term **"lobotomy"** can be used to describe H.M.'s surgery.

    A: _____

2. Assessment of the amnesic effects of bilateral medial-temporal-lobe lesions in animals seems to rule out the

    theory that _____ damage by itself is responsible for medial-temporal-lobe amnesia.

3. Number these five phases of posttraumatic amnesia from 1 to 5 to indicate their chronological order.

    ___. blow to the head
    ___. period covered by the retrograde amnesia
    ___. period of coma
    ___. period of confusion and anterograde amnesia
    ___. period during which normal memories are formed but there is still retrograde amnesia for the brief
         period before the blow

4. **True or False:** The **repetition priming** test has proven most useful in studying medial-temporal-lobe amnesia in monkeys.

    A: _____

Next to the following seven statements, write the name of one of the following tests: digit span test, digit span +1 test, block-tapping memory-span +1 test, matching-to-sample test, mirror-drawing test, rotary-pursuit test, incomplete-pictures test

5. After 25 trials, H.M. could still only do 7.

    A: _____

6. H.M. did not learn a sequence one more than his normal span when the same sequence was presented 12 times.

    A: _____

7. H.M.'s time-on-target increased over 12 daily sessions although he did not recall the sessions from one day to the next.

    A: _____

8. There are five sets of cards. H.M. showed improvement when the test was unexpectedly repeated an hour later.

    A: _____

9. His score was 6, which is well within the normal range of performance for healthy subjects.

    A: _____

10. Although the initial research focused on the hippocampus, current evidence from a variety of animal studies suggests that damage to the _____ is to blame for the problems with object recognition that are produced following bilateral medial-temporal-lobe lesions.

11. One interpretation of the "retrograde amnesia" gradient observed in Korsakoff patients is that it reflects the progressive worsening of what is really _____ amnesia.

12. Patient R.B. displayed clear damage to the _____ subfield of the hippocampus following an ischemic accident. .

13. At autopsy, the brains of Alzheimer patients display three striking forms of pathology: neuronal degeneration, _____ plaques, and _____ in the neural cytoplasm.

14. There is a major reduction in the neurotransmitter _____ in the brains of Alzheimer patients.

15. Gradients of retrograde amnesia can be studied in laboratory animals by administering _____ to groups of animals at different intervals after a learning trial.

16. The nonrecurring-items delayed nonmatching-to-sample apparatus that was developed for rats is called the _____ box.

17. Much of the research on implicit memory has employed the repetition- _____ task.

18. **True or False:** There seem to be two fundamentally different kinds of memories, <u>retrograde</u> memories and <u>anterograde</u> memories, which are measured by implicit and explicit tests of memory, respectively.

    A: _____

19. According to Lashley, the _____ is the hypothetical change in the brain responsible for storing a memory.

20. The memory deficits observed in patients with Alzheimer's disease or with Korsakoff's syndrome are similar in that there is _____ amnesia in both groups of patients.

21. The _____ is comprised of the entorhinal and perirhinal cortex.

22. The activity of _____ in the hippocampus emerges as the rat familiarizes itself with the environment; the subsequent activity of these cells indicates where the rat thinks it is in the test environment.

23. _____ is a disorder common in people who have consumed large quantities of alcohol for prolonged periods of time.

24. **True or False:** The <u>dorsomedial nucleus of the</u> thalamus plays an important role in memories about the emotional aspects of an experience.

    A: _____

## C. Diagrams.

**Figure 1.** Identify the 6 memory-related structures illustrated in this coronal section of the diencephalon and temporal lobe.

A) _____

B) _____

C) _____

D) _____

E) _____

F) _____

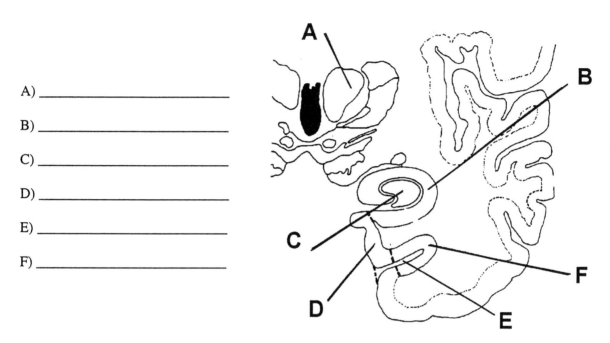

## D. Short Answer Section. In no more than 5 sentences, answer each of the following questions.

1. Compare the role of the hippocampus, the rhinal cortex, and the inferotemporal cortex in memory function.

2.  Describe Lashley's search for the engram, and what his efforts suggested about the neural basis of learning and memory.

3.  Describe Nadel and Moscovitch's (1997) theory linking the hippocampus, consolidation, and episodic memory.

4.  What are the key psychological and neural differences between explicit/declarative memories and implicit/procedural memories?

**Mark your answers to the practice examination; the correct answers follow.  On the basis of your performance, plan the final stages of your studying.**

# Answers to the Practice Examination

## A. Multiple Choice Section

| | | | |
|---|---|---|---|
| 1. b | 6. d | 11. c | 16. a, b |
| 2. c | 7. d | 12. b, c | 17. a, b, c |
| 3. a, c | 8. a, b, c | 13. b | 18. b, c |
| 4. c | 9. a, b, d | 14. d | 19. b |
| 5. a, b | 10. c | 15. b | 20. a |

## B. Modified True/False and Fill-in-the-Blank Section

1. False; lobectomy
2. hippocampal
3. 2, 1, 3, 4, 5
4. False; nonrecurring-items delayed-nonmatching-to-sample
5. digit-span + 1 task
6. block-tapping memory-span
7. rotary-pursuit
8. incomplete-pictures
9. digit-span
10. rhinal cortex
11. anterograde
12. CA 1
13. amyloid, neurofibrillary tangles
14. acetylcholine
15. ECS
16. Mumby
17. priming
18. False; procedural and declarative, respectively
19. engram
20. retrograde
21. rhinal cortex
22. place cells
23. Korsakoff's syndrome
24. False; amygdala

## C. Diagrams

Figure 1.  A) Dorsomedial Nucleus of Thalamus  B) Hippocampus  C) Dentate Gyrus  D) Entorhinal Cortex  E) Rhinal Fissure  F) Perirhinal Cortex

## D. Short Answer Section

1. Mention the hippocampus' role in forming spatial memories; the rhinal cortex's role in developing object recognition; and the inferotemporal cortex's role in memory storage.

2. Mention that Lashley looked at the effects of brain lesions on an animal's memory for events prior to the surgery; that his search suggested that all cortical areas participated equally in memory, a conclusion that slowed our understanding of the localization of learning and memory to specific parts of the brain.

3. Mention that these researchers theorize that the hippocampus is involved in the storage of specific episodic memories; consolidation involves repeated activation of related hippocampal circuits, which make the original memory easier to recall and more difficult to disrupt.

4. Mention that explicit memories can be expressed by declaration (declarative memory), whereas implicit memories are not available to conscious awareness and must be implied by improved skill on various test procedures (procedural memory); that explicit memory is much more sensitive to brain damage, being changed following damage to various temporal, frontal and diencephalic structures; implicit memory is compromised in Alzheimer's patients.

---

# Chapter 15

## NEUROPLASTICITY: DEVELOPMENT, LEARNING, AND RECOVERY FROM BRAIN DAMAGE

---

## I.    Jeopardy Study Items

*With reference to Chapter 15 of BIOPSYCHOLOGY, write the correct answer to each of the following questions and the correct question for each of the following answers.*

1.    What is the simple systems approach to the study of neuroplasticity?  What is its main advantage?

2.    In addition to cell multiplication, what three processes are responsible for the development of organisms into distinct entities?

3.                                          A:  This is called the neural plate.

4.                                          A:  This is called the neural tube.

5.    What does totipotential mean?

6.    With the development of the neural plate, the cells of the dorsal ectoderm lose their totipotency.  What does this mean?

7.  What is induction?

8.                                          A: This usually occurs in the ventricular zone of the neural tube.

9.                                          A: These are called stem cells.

10. What are radial glial cells?

11. What is tangential migration?

12. Describe the migration of cells from the ventricular zone to the subventricular, intermediate, and cortical areas.

13.                                         A: This is called the inside-out pattern of cortical development.

14. What is the neural crest? Why is it of special interest to scientists who study neural migration?

15. What are neural cell-adhesion molecules?

16.                                         A: This is thought to be mediated by neural cell-adhesion molecules.

17.    What is the growth cone?  Why is it important to the study of neural development?

18.    Describe the key idea underlying the chemoaffinity hypothesis of axonal development.

19.    Describe two findings that support the chemoaffinity hypothesis of axonal growth.

20.    Describe two problems with the chemoaffinity hypothesis of axonal growth.

21.    Describe the blueprint hypothesis of neural development.

22.    How do pioneer growth cones find their targets?

23.                                              A:  This is called fasciculation.

24.    Describe two problems with the blueprint  hypothesis of axonal growth.

25.    What is the topographic-gradient hypothesis?

26. How does regeneration in the visual system of the frog support the topographic-gradient hypothesis of axon development?

27. What three findings suggest that developing neurons die because of their failure to compete successfully for a life-promoting factor from their target?

28.                                        A: This is released by the targets of sympathetic neurons and helps to promote their survival.

29. What is the difference between necrosis and apoptosis?

30. What is the main effect of cell death on synaptic organization?

31. What is the key idea that governs the effects of experience on neural development?

32. Describe the competitive nature of synapse rearrangement as demonstrated by studies of early monocular deprivation.

33. Describe the competitive nature of synapse organization as demonstrated by studies of motoneuron innervation of muscle fibers.

34. Describe Knudsen and Brainard's (1991) demonstration of an interaction between auditory and visual topographic maps during neural development.

35. List 3 different mechanisms by which experience might alter neural development.

Chapter 15

36. Define learning and memory.

37. How does the Aplysia gill-withdrawal reflex work?

38.                                         A: This is called *nonassociative learning.*

39.                                         A: This is called habituation.

40. What did researchers first discover about the neural
    mechanism underlying habituation of the gill withdrawal
    reflex in *Aplysia*?

41. What is the basis for the decline in motoneuron activity
    in *Aplysia* during the habituation of its gill reflex?

42.                                         A: This is called sensitization.

43. How does presynaptic facilitation mediate sensitization?

44. What kind of associative learning has been
    demonstrated in *Aplysia*?

45. What is the difference between sensitization and
    Pavlovian conditioning?

46. Where do the changes underlying Pavlovian conditioning
    of the *Aplysia* gill withdrawal reflex occur...
    presynaptically or postsynaptically or ??

47. What are second messengers?  Give an example of one
    second messenger pathway.

48. What kinds of structural changes are produced in *Aplysia*
    neurons following long-term habituation?  long-term
    sensitization?

49.                                     A:  This is called long-term potentiation.

50. Where has LTP been most frequently studied?

51. What two characteristics make LTP so useful to Hebb's
    hypothesis about the neural bases of learning and
    memory?

52.                                     A:  This is called Hebb's postulate for learning.

53.                                     A:  This is called the NMDA receptor.

54. What quality makes the NMDA receptor unique?  Why
    is it important to the induction of LTP?

55. Why is the requirement for cooccurence of activation in
    LTP such an interesting and important feature of LTP?

Chapter 15

56.                                          A: These have been shown to block the induction of LTP.

57. Why are dendritic spines important to the specificity of
    LTP?

58.                                          A: These have been shown to block the long-term
                                             maintenance of LTP.

59.                                          A: This is called nitric oxide.

60.                                          A: This is called an axotomy.

61. What is the difference between anterograde and
    retrograde degeneration?

62. Why does anterograde degeneration occur so quickly?

63. What is phagocytosis? What two cell types are
    responsible for this process?

64.                                          A: This is called transneuronal degeneration.

65. What factors are required for successful regeneration in
    the PNS?

66. Why is regeneration more likely to occur in the
    mammalian PNS than in the CNS?

67.                                                    A: This is called collateral sprouting.

68. What is the evidence that collateral sprouting is elicited by some factor released by the denervated target tissue?

69. Why are primary sensory and primary motor cortices ideally suited to study neural reorganization?

70. What 3 manipulations can be used to cause the reorganization of primary sensory cortex in mammals?

71. How does motor cortex reorganize itself in adult animals?

72.                                                    A: These mechanisms include a change in the strength of existing connections or collateral sprouting.

73. Describe the apparent role of the basal forebrain in neural reorganization of primary auditory cortex.

74. What three general conclusions have emerged from research on the recovery of function?

75. How can rehabilitative training assist in the recovery of function be promoted following neural damage?

76. What 2 strategies have been devised to control the application of neurotrophins in the treatment of brain injury?

77. Describe the use of PNS nerve implants into the CNS to promote *functional* regeneration in the CNS.

78.                                                      A:  This is called autotransplantation.

79. Compare the effectiveness of adrenal medulla implants and fetal substantia nigra implants in the treatment of Parkinson's Disease.

80. What are the two strategies adopted for the use of neurotransplantation to treat CNS disorders?

---

Once you have completed the jeopardy study items, study them.  Practice bidirectional studying; make sure that you know the correct answer to every question and the correct question for every answer.

---

## II.    Essay Study Questions

*Using Chapter 15 of BIOPSYCHOLOGY, write an outline of the answer to each of the following essay study questions.*

1.   Describe the five stages of neural development:  (1) induction of the neural plate, (2) neural proliferation, (3) migration and aggregation, (4) axon growth and (5) synapse rearrangement.

2.   Compare and contrast the chemoaffinity hypothesis, the blueprint hypothesis, and the topographic gradient hypothesis of axonal growth and development; give an example of research supporting each hypothesis as well as problems with each hypothesis.

3.   Describe the neural basis of the following kinds of learning in the Aplysia gill-withdrawal circuit:  habituation, sensitization, and Pavlovian conditioning.

4. What is LTP? Describe the six lines of indirect evidence that suggest the physiological changes underlying LTP may be comparable to those that store memories.

5. Compare and contrast the phenomena of LTP and conditioning of the gill withdrawal reflex in *Aplysia*.

6. Describe the various categories of neuronal and transneuronal degeneration.

7. How do adult motor and sensory systems reorganize themselves after damage?

8. Describe the evidence that neurotransplantation might be effective against Parkinson's disease. What is the current status of adrenal medulla autotransplantation?

9. Our understanding of the mechanisms for the maintenance and expression of long-term potentiation have advanced on three fronts. Comment on each of these areas of research.

> **When you have answered the essay study questions, memorize your outlines to prepare for your upcoming examination.**

## III. Practice Examination

After completing most of your studying of Chapter 15, but at least 24 hours before your formal examination, write the following practice examination.

**A. Multiple-Choice Section.** Circle the correct answer for each question; *REMEMBER that some questions may have more than one correct answer.*

1. Which layer of the neural tube displays the inside-out pattern of development?

   a. cortical plate
   b. intermediate zone
   c. ventricular zone
   d. marginal zone

2. At the tip of each growing axon is:

   a. a synapse.
   b. a structure with filopodia.
   c. a growth cone.
   d. an astrocyte.

3. According to the blueprint hypothesis, only pioneer growth cones need to be able to travel to the correct destination; the other growth cones in a developing tract get there by:

   a. festination.
   b. blue prints.
   c. nerve growth factor.
   d. fasciculation.

4. Apoptosis is:

   a. a breakfast food with sprinkles and icing on top.
   b. active cell death.
   c. always dangerous, as it leads to potentially harmful inflammation.
   d. responsible for pruning tissues by removing cells in a safe, neat and orderly way.

5. Early monocular deprivation produces significant reductions in the ability of the deprived eye to activate cortical neurons:

   a. within 2-3 months of the deprivation.
   b. within days of the deprivation.
   c. by reducing the axonal branching of lateral geniculate neurons into layer IV of visual cortex.
   d. by reducing the release of transmitter by lateral geniculate neurons that project into layer IV of visual cortex.

6. Pavlovian conditioning of the Aplysia gill-withdrawal reflex involves:

   a. a noxious stimulus.
   b. a conditional stimulus such as a light touch of the siphon.
   c. alterations in 2nd messenger systems.
   d. increased protein synthesis in the neuron cell body.

7. LTP and learning/memory processes are similar in that:

   a. they are associative phenomena.
   b. they last a long time.
   c. they only take place in the hippocampus.
   d. they can only be demonstrated *in vivo*.

8. Despite the difficulties in studying recovery of function, the following general conclusions have emerged:

   a. Recovery of function is less common than is generally believed.
   b. Small lesions are more likely than large lesions to be associated with recovery.
   c. Recovery is more likely in young patients.
   d. brain damage is not as detrimental to behavior as one might expect.

9. Collateral sprouting following neural damage is:

   a. seen in regenerating axons.
   b. seen in healthy axons that are adjacent to a damaged axon.
   c. thought to be triggered by some factor released by the target tissue.
   d. due to growth cones.

10. Primary sensory cortex is:

   a. very dynamic, changing its organization depending upon the nature of the stimuli it is processing.
   b. organized topographically.
   c. dynamically organized in developing organisms, and becoming fixed in adult life.
   d. largest in trained musicians.

11. Exogenous neurotrophins may be delivered into the brain via:

   a. intracerebral injection.
   b. genetically altered viruses.
   c. growth cones.
   d. stem cells.

12. Functional *regeneration* in the CNS has been accomplished by:

   a. transplanting fetal cells into the brain.
   b. autotransplantation.
   c. transplanting sections of myelinated PNS nerves into the CNS.
   d. injection of genetically altered viruses.

13. Transplantation of dopamine-containing fetal neurons into the striatum:

   a. has been very effective in the treatment of Parkinson's disease.
   b. is most effective when the cells are derived from adrenal medulla.
   c. is most effective when the cells are derived from an early-term fetus.
   d. has only been successful in nonhuman primates.

**B. Modified True-False and Fill-in-the Blank Section.** If the statement is true, write TRUE in the blank provided. If the statement is false, write FALSE as well as the word or words that will make the statement true if they replaced the highlighted word or words in the original statement. If the statement is incomplete, write the word or words that will complete it.

1. Why have many researchers interested in neuroplasticity focused on invertebrates and simple vertebrates? The answer in one word is "_____SIMPLICITY_____."

2. Write neural tube, neural groove, and neural plate in their correct developmental sequence.
   _____neural plate → neural grove → neural tube_____

3. Prior to the development of the neural plate, the cells of the dorsal ectoderm are said to be
   _____Totipotential_____; that is, they can develop into any kind of cell.

4. The development of the neural plate appears to be induced by the underlying _____mesoderm_____.

5. **True or False:** Most cell division in the neural tube occurs in the **neural crest**.
   A: _____ventricularzone_____

6. Glial cells and interneurons develop in the _____ zone of the neural tube.

7. Migrating neurons move outward along _____radial glial_____ cells to their destinations.

8. The assumption that co-occurrence of activity is a physiological necessity for learning is often referred to as
   _____.

9. **True or False:** According to the chemoaffinity hypothesis, the main guiding force underlying axonal migration appears to the growth cones' attraction to **neural cell-adhesion molecules**.
   A: _____post synaptic Target chemicals_____

*Three lines of evidence support the topographic gradient hypothesis. Complete the following three statements.*

10. Axons regenerating from intact frog retinas to lesioned optic tectums _____
    _____.

11. Axons regenerating from the remaining portions of lesioned frog retinas to intact optic tectums _____
    _____.

12. Synaptic connections between eyes and optic tectums are established long before either reaches full size. As they grow, the initially established synaptic connections _____
    _____.

13. __neurotrophins__ are life-preserving chemicals that are supplied to a neuron by its target tissue.

14. **True or False:** The early function of neurotransmitters like **the monoamines** play an important role in the effects of experience on normal neural development.

    **A:** _____

15. In a muscle fiber that is innervated by two motoneurons, the neuron that is most _____active_____ will eventually take precedence over the other motoneuron.

16. Name two types of nonassociative learning.

    a. _____
    b. _____

17. The Aplysia gill-withdrawal reflex is commonly elicited in experiments by touching or shocking the _____.

18. **True or False:** During **habituation,** the responsiveness of motor neurons to neurotransmitter released by sensory neurons does not decline.

    **A:** _____

19. During habituation of the gill withdrawal reflex in *Aplysia,* the number of action potentials elicited in the _____ by each successive touch declines.

20. _____ is a general increase in an animal's responsiveness to stimuli following a noxious stimulus.

21. **True or False:** **Sensitization** results from a decrease in the amount of neurotransmitter released by the siphon sensory neurons in response to their own action potentials.

    **A:** _____

22. Pavlovian conditioning of the Aplysia gill-withdrawal reflex can be thought of as a special case of _____.

23. As demonstrated by Chen and Bailey, the structural changes that underlie the formation of long-term memories in *Aplysia* during habituation include _____.

24. The long-term facilitation of synaptic transmission that underlies LTP is similar in certain respects to the facilitation that has been presumed to be the basis of _____.

25. One important discovery about LTP is that it requires cooccurence of active inputs such as would be required during _____ conditioning.

Chapter 15

26. The _____ receptor is a glutamate receptor subtype that is thought to play an important role in LTP.

27. The _____ of activity in presynaptic and postsynaptic neurons is the critical factor in all forms of associative neural plasticity.

28. Recent evidence suggests that the specificity of LTP is attributable to changes localized to the

_____ of the postsynaptic neurons.

29. The degeneration of the distal segment of an axon is commonly referred to as
_____anterograde_____ degeneration.

30. True or false: If CNS tissue is transplanted to a corresponding position in the host, it will **rarely establish** connections with the surrounding tissue.

    A: _____

31. **True or False:** Following amputation of an arm, researchers have found that the somatosensory cortex for the arm has **degenerated.** reorganized around remaining inputs

    A: _____

32. The likelihood of recovery of function following damage in the CNS is greatest if the lesion is
_____small_____ and the patient is _____young_____.

33. After cutting the optic nerve, Aguayo and his colleagues have promoted the regeneration of rat CNS neurons by implanting a _____Schwan cell_____ from the PNS between the retina and the superior colliculus.

34. Bilateral transplantation of _____Fetal dopaminergic_____ cells has proven effective in alleviating parkinsonian symptoms in both animal models and human beings.

35. Injections of _____MPTP_____ into primates causes severe Parkinson's disease.

## C. Diagrams

**Figure 1.** Identify the following structures of the developing nervous system.

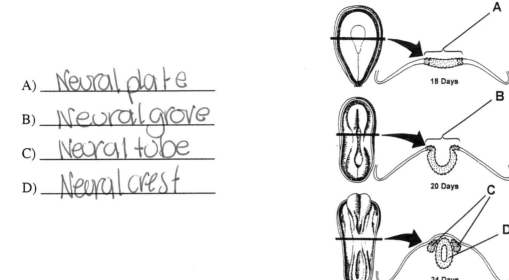

A) _Neural plate_

B) _Neural grove_

C) _Neural tube_

D) _Neural crest_

**Figure 2.** Identify each stage of neural degeneration.

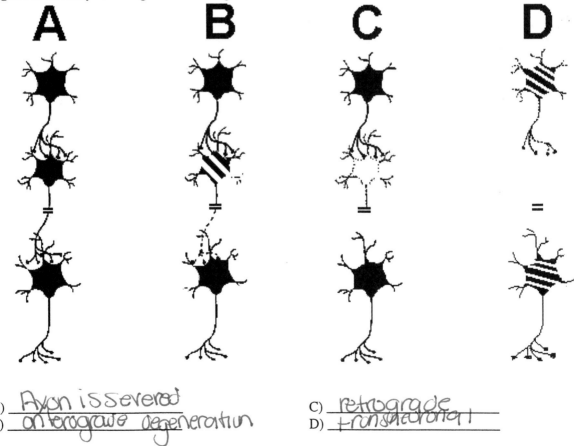

A) _Axon is severed_

B) _anterograde degeneration_

C) _retrograde_

D) _transneuronal_

**D. Short Answer Section.** In no more than 5 sentences, answer each of the following questions.

1. Two mechanisms have been proposed to account for the reorganization of neural circuits that is observed in adult mammals after damage. What are these mechanisms, and what evidence supports each mechanism?

2. Long-term potentiation and learning and memory processes are phenomenologically similar in many different ways; describe four areas of similarity.

**Mark your answers to the practice examination; the correct answers follow. On the basis of your performance, plan the final stages of your studying.**

8. What is the dichotic listening test?

9. Why does the superior ear on the dichotic listening test indicate the dominance of the contralateral hemisphere?

10. What have PET and fMRI studies revealed about brain activity during language-related tasks like reading?

11.                                    A: These people are referred to as sinestrals.

12. What is the relation between handedness and speech laterality for dextrals, sinestrals, and ambidextrous people?

13. What did McGlone conclude about differences in laterality of function between women and men?

14. Why was the corpus callosum considered something of a paradox in the early 1950s?

15. Why did Sperry have to cut the optic chiasm of his feline subjects in his early studies on laterality of function?

16.                                              A: This is called a scotoma.

17. What did Meyers and Sperry conclude about the
    function of the corpus callosum, based upon their work
    with cats?

18. Why is there no transfer of fine tactual and motor
    information in split-brain monkeys?

19.                                              A: This surgery helped to prevent the spread of epileptic
                                                 discharges in human beings.

20. Why is the optic chiasm never cut in human split-brain
    surgery?

21. Why are visual stimuli commonly presented for only 0.1
    second to the subjects in human split-brain studies?

22. What is the key difference between the results of split-
    brain studies done in animals and those done in humans?

23. What evidence supports the idea that the hemispheres of
    the human brain can function independently?

24.                                              A: This is called cross-cueing.

25. What evidence is there that the two hemispheres of a
    split-brain patient can learn two different things at the
    same time?

26. What is the "helping-hand" phenomenon?


27.                                        A: This was developed by Zaidel to compare the abilities of the hemispheres of split-brain patients


28. Why is the idea that the left hemisphere is dominant considered obsolete?


29.                                        A: This side of the brain is better at controlling ipsilateral movements.


30.                                        A: This means to "tactually investigate".


31. If you had a split-brain operation, which hand would you want to use to tactually identify something? Why?


32.                                        A: This study suggests that emotions, but not visual information, are transferred between hemispheres in split-brain patients.


33. Why did Kimura conclude that the right hemisphere was superior for the perception of melodies?


34. Describe why your right hemisphere "thinks like a rat" in certain tests of memory.


35. Describe some of the evidence that suggests that the right hemisphere is capable of rudimentary language tasks.

36.                                    A:  These structures include the planum temporale, Heschel's gyrus, and the frontal operculum.

37.                                    A: This is associated with perfect pitch perception.

38.  What are the analytic and synthetic modes of thinking?

39.  What is Kimura's sensorimotor theory of cerebral lateralization?

40.  "Cerebral lateralization is a uniquely human characteristic."  Discuss this statement.

41.  What is the difference between language laterality and language localization?

42.                                    A:  This is called the Wernicke-Geschwind model of language.

43.  Where are Broca's and Wernicke's areas?

44.                                    A:  This is called Broca's aphasia.

45.                                    A:  This is also called word salad.

46. What is conduction aphasia?

47. What kind of language deficits are produced by damage
    to the left angular gyrus?

48. What is the difference between a serial model and a
    parallel model of brain function?

49. Describe the series of events that occur in your cortex
    when you are reading out loud, according to the
    Wernicke-Geschwind model of language.

50. What have CAT and MRI studies told us about the cause
    of language-related disorders?

51. What is a global aphasia?

52.                                    A: These areas include the left basal ganglia, the left
                                       subcortical white matter, or the left thalamus.

53. Why is electrical stimulation such a useful tool in the
    study of the cerebral localization of language?

54.                                    A: These are called phonemes.

55.                                    A: This part of the brain seems to underlie the phonological
                                       analysis of language.

56.                                        A: This is called dyslexia.

57. Describe the dual-route parallel model of reading out
    loud.

58. What is the difference between surface dyslexia and
    deep dyslexia?

59. What evidence is there that nonlexical language skills
    are localized to the left hemisphere?

60. Describe some of the brain abnormalities associated with
    dyslexia.

61. Describe the paired-subtraction technique used by
    Petersen and his colleagues to study language
    localization using PET imaging.

62.                                        A: This appears to be the location where semantic processing
                                           of verb association occurs.

63. Describe the 3 key findings of Bavalier et al.'s fMRI
    study of cortical activation during language tasks.

64. Based on PET, fMRI, and stimulation studies, where are
    the functions that were traditionally ascribed to Broca's
    area and Wernicke's area located?

---

**Once you have completed the jeopardy study items, study them. Practice bidirectional studying; make sure
that you know the correct answer to every question and the correct question for every answer.**

## II.    Essay Study Questions

*Using Chapter 16 of BIOPSYCHOLOGY, write an outline of the answer to each of the following essay study questions.*

1. Compare and contrast the analytic-semantic theory, the motor theory, and the linguistic theory of cerebral asymmetry.

2. Discuss the statement "Laterality of function is statistical, not absolute."

3. Describe Myers and Sperry's ground-breaking 1953 experimental study of split-brain cats. How did the results of these studies compare to Sperry and Gazzaniga's later work with human split-brain patients?

4.  Summarize the results of tests with split-brain patients. What do these results suggest about the function of the corpus callosum and the organization of our brains?

5.  What is dyslexia? Discuss the behavioral and possible anatomical differences between deep and surface dyslexia.

6.  Identify the seven key components of the Wernicke-Geschwind model of language. According to this model, how were the different parts of this model supposed to work when a person is repeating a spoken work?

7.  Briefly describe what we currently know about the role of each component of the Wernicke-Geschwind model of language.

8.  Describe the paired-subtraction technique developed by Petersen and his colleagues to use PET and fMRI images to study the localization of language functions in the brain.

9. Compare the sodium amytal test and the dichotic listening test of language laterality.

When you have answered the essay study questions, memorize your outlines to prepare for your upcoming examination.

## III.    Practice Examination

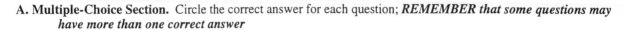

*After completing most of your studying of Chapter 16, but at least 24 hours before your formal examination, write the following practice examination.*

**A. Multiple-Choice Section.**  Circle the correct answer for each question; *REMEMBER that some questions may have more than one correct answer*

1.  This unknown country doctor is now recognized as the first person to have presented an academic paper on the topic of lateralization of brain function:

    a.  Dax
    b.  Broca
    c.  Geschwind
    d.  Wernicke

2.  Which of the following is not normally cut during a conventional commissurotomy performed on a human epileptic?

    a.  optic chiasm
    b.  anterior commissure
    c.  hippocampal commissure
    d.  corpus callosum

3.  Which of the following did not occur in the ground-breaking 1953 split-brain experiment of Myers and Sperry?

    a.  Some cats had their corpus callosums transected.
    b.  Some cats had their optic chiasms transected.
    c.  All cats were trained to fixate on a point.
    d.  Some cats had both their optic chiasms and their corpus callosums transected.

4.  In Meyers and Sperry's groundbreaking experiment, the performance of one group of well-trained trained cats fell to chance levels when they were tested with the untrained eye.  The cats in this group had their:

    a.  optic chiasms transected.
    b.  corpus callosums transected.
    c.  epileptic foci destroyed.
    d.  memories impaired.

5.  Which of Sperry's colleagues bore the primary responsibility for testing the first group of commissurotomized human beings?

    a.  Vogel
    b.  Bogen
    c.  Bryden
    d.  Gazzaniga

6. In a well-known study, split-brain patients performed the chimeric figures test. When asked what they had seen, they:

   a. verbally reported seeing whole faces rather than chimeric figures.
   b. verbally reported that they had seen a whole face that was a completed version of the half that had been in their right visual field.
   c. pointed to a whole face that was a completed version of the half that had been in the left visual field.
   d. were confused.

7. In tests of language competence, the right hemisphere of a split-brain subject tends to have:

   a. no language skills.
   b. a completely intact set of language skills that is normally overshadowed by the left hemisphere.
   c. the language skills of a two year old.
   d. the language skills of a preschooler.

8. Damage to which of the following structures has been associated with alexia and agraphia?

   a. angular gyrus
   b. arcuate fasciculus
   c. Broca's area
   d. Wernicke's area

9. The Wernicke-Geschwind model of language:

   a. is a serial model of brain function.
   b. is a parallel model of brain function.
   c. integrated the earlier work of Broca, Wernicke and Dejerine.
   d. refuted the earlier work of Broca, Wernicke and Dejerine.

10. Small surgical lesions that selectively destroy Broca's area or the angular gyrus, or selectively transect the arcuate fasciculus:

    a. produce Broca's aphasia.
    b. produce conduction aphasia.
    c. have little, if any, lasting effect on language- related abilities.
    d. produce Wernicke's aphasia

11. Ojemann and his colleagues have found that:

    a. stimulation of Wernicke's area can induce a temporary aphasia.
    b. areas of cortex at which stimulation could interfere with language extended far beyond the boundaries of the Wernicke-Geschwind model.
    c. all language abilities were represented bilaterally.
    d. that each patient displayed roughly the same neural organization of language abilities.

12. According to Mateer and Cameron, cortical stimulation in the area of the lateral fissure tends to disrupt:

    a. speech production.
    b. analysis of speech sounds.
    c. analysis of speech structure.
    d. analysis of speech meaning.

13. Which of the following is considered to be part of Wernicke's area?

    a. Heschl's gyrus
    b. frontal operculum
    c. planum temporale
    d. angular gyrus

14. In Kimura's tests of musical ability, the right ear/left hemisphere was better able to:

    a. perceive melodies.
    b. perceive digits.
    c. perceive single notes.
    d. perceive complex rhythms.

15. According to Peterson's dual-route theory of language, during the performance of a highly practiced verbal response neural processing moves from:

    a. sensory cortex to motor cortex through the association cortex of the lateral fissure.
    b. sensory cortex to motor cortex through the frontal and cingulate cortex.
    c. sensory cortex to motor cortex through the corpus callosum.
    d. sensory cortex to motor cortex through the optic chiasm.

16. Coltheart proposed that the left hemisphere of the brain:

    a. was the language center of the brain.
    b. contained the neural mechanisms mediating the lexical procedure of reading.
    c. contained the neural mechanisms mediating the nonlexical procedure of reading.
    d. mediates the pronunciation of nonwords and the ability to read on the basis of translating letters into sounds.

17. The only observation from lesion studies that is consistent with the Wernicke-Geschwind model of language is that:

    a. large lesions to the arcuate fasciculus effectively disconnected Wernicke's area from Broca's area.
    b. large lesions to Broca's area produced Broca's aphasia.
    c. large lesions to the posterior brain were more likely to be associated with articulation deficits.
    d. large lesions to the anterior brain were more likely to be associated with articulation deficits.

18. Commissurotomies are done in human beings to:

    a. allow their brains to do twice as much work.
    b. control their epileptic seizures.
    c. study the neural bases of language.
    d. control hydrocephaly.

**B. Modified True-False and Fill-in-the Blank Section.** If the statement is true, write TRUE in the blank provided. If the statement is false, write FALSE as well as the word or words that will make the statement true if they replaced the highlighted word or words in the original statement. If the statement is incomplete, write the word or words that will complete it.

1. Broca's area is in the inferior _prefrontal_ cortex of the left hemisphere.

2. **True** or False: **Aphasia** is almost always associated with damage to the left hemisphere.

   **A:** _____

3. Although the symptoms of apraxia are bilateral, they are usually produced by unilateral _left_ - hemisphere lesions.

4. Sinestrals are _left_ -handers.

5. The _sodium amytal test_ test is an invasive test of speech lateralization that is often given to patients prior to neurosurgery.

6. The _dichotic listening_ test is a noninvasive test of language lateralization that was developed by Kimura.

7. **True** or **False:** Left-handed subjects tend to have language lateralized to the **right** hemisphere of their brain.

   **A:** _____

8. The largest cerebral commissure is called the _____.

9. In order to compare the reading ability of a split-brain patient's left and right hemispheres, it is necessary to use a device such as the _Z lens_ lens, which was developed by Zaidel.

10. In lab animals that have had a commissurotomy, visual information can be presented to the left hemisphere without the right hemisphere being aware of following surgical transection of the _optic chiasm_ .

11. **True** or False: The **planum temporale** is largest on the left side of the brain.

   **A:** _____

12. Although the two hemispheres of a split-brain patient cannot directly communicate, they can sometimes influence one another indirectly by a method called _cross cueing_ .

Chapter 16

13. Imagine that you are examining a split-brain patient. An image of a pencil is flashed in the left visual field of the person, and an image of an apple is simultaneously flashed in the right visual field . Answer "true" or "false" to each of the following statements.

    a. The subject said that they had seen an apple. __T__

    b. When requested to feel several out-of-sight objects with their left hand and to select the object that they had seen, they picked a pencil. __T__

    c. When identifying the object that they had seen by simultaneously feeling two groups of out-of-sight objects, one group with each hand, they picked two pencils. __F__

14. **True or False:** According to Levy and Sperry, the **left hemisphere** thinks in a synthetic mode.

        RIGHT

        A: _____

15. **True or False:** According to Kimura, the **left hemisphere** is specialized for the control of fine motor movements, of which speech is but one particularly important example.

        A: _____

16. "Lateralization" refers to the relative control of a behavior by the left or the right hemisphere; in contrast,

"_____" refers to the location within the hemispheres of the neural

circuits responsible for the behavior.

17. Using the Wernicke-Geshwind model of language to guide your answers, write "Broca's", "Wernicke's", or "conduction" in each of the following blanks.

    a. a veritable word salad: __W__ aphasia

    b. damage just posterior to the left primary auditory area: __W__ aphasia

    c. damage to the arcuate fasciculus of the left hemisphere: __C__ aphasia

    d. damage to the left prefrontal lobe just anterior to the left primary motor face area of the motor homunculus: __B__ aphasia

    e. primarily receptive: __W__ aphasia

    f. primarily expressive: __B__ aphasia

18. **True or False:** The brains of female humans are **more lateralized than** the brains of males humans.

        A: _____

19. The Wernicke-Geschwind model is not a parallel model; it is a __serial__ model.

20. CT-scan studies have revealed that large anterior lesions of the left hemisphere are more likely to produce deficits in language _expression_ than are large posterior lesions, and that large posterior lesions of the left hemisphere are more likely to produce deficits in language _____ than are large anterior lesions.

21. There are two different procedures for reading aloud: a _lexical_ procedure, which is based on memories of the pronunciations of specific words, and a _nonlexical_ procedure, which is based on memories of general rules of pronunciation.

22. **True or False:** For the majority of people, there is a slight tendency for words presented to the right ear to be recognized **more readily** than those presented to in the left ear.

    A: _____

23. In surface dyslexia, the _nonlexical_ procedure remains intact while the _lexical_ procedure is disturbed; thus patients with surface dyslexia have difficulty in pronouncing irregular words like "yacht" and "sew" but have no difficulty in pronouncing regular nonwords such as "spleemer" and "twipple."

24. Petersen and his colleagues used a _____ technique to study the neural bases of language using PET images.

25. **True or False:** Petersen and his colleagues found that the lateral fissure was **activated** when subjects had to associate a verb with a noun that they had been presented with.

    A: _____

26. The right hemisphere of the human brain is best at tasks such as spatial ability, _musical_ ability, and in the experience of _emotion_ .

27. The ability of each hemisphere to simultaneously and independently engage in visual completion has been demonstrated using the _chimeric figures_ test.

28. **True or False:** McGlone found that **male victims** of unilateral strokes had deficits on both the verbal subtests and the performance subtests of the WAIS, regardless of which side the stroke was on.

    A: _FEMALE VICTIMS_

## C. Diagrams.

**Figure 1.** Label the highlighted areas of the Wernicke-Geschwind model of language.

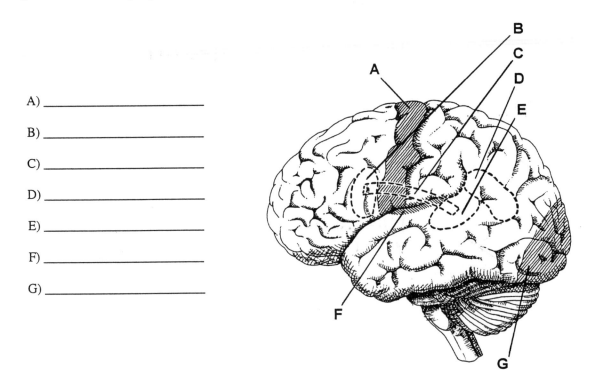

A) _____

B) _____

C) _____

D) _____

E) _____

F) _____

G) _____

**Figure 2.** Identify these language-related areas of neuroanatomical asymmetry.

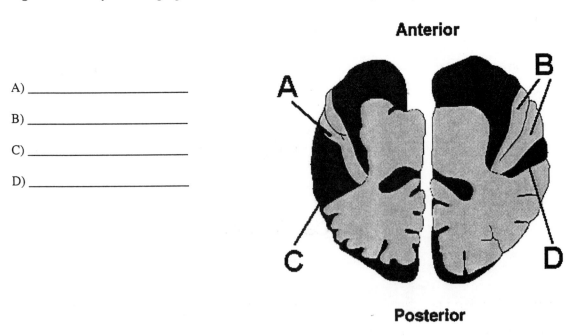

A) _____

B) _____

C) _____

D) _____

---

# Chapter 17

## THE BIOPSYCHOLOGY OF
## STRESS AND ILLNESS

---

## I.    Jeopardy Study Items

*With reference to Chapter 17 of BIOPSYCHOLOGY, write the correct answer to each of the following questions and the correct question for each of the following answers.*

1.                                              A:  This means emotional.

2.                                              A:  This was titled *The Expression of Emotion in Man and Animals.*

3.  What are the 3 main parts of Darwin's theory of the evolution of emotional expression?

4.                                              A:  This is called the *principle of antithesis.*

5.  What was the key idea behind the James-Lange theory of emotion?

6.                                              A:  This theory viewed emotional experience and emotional expression as parallel processes that are not causally related.

7. What is sham rage, and what did it suggest about the
   hypothalamus?

8. According to Papez, what is the function of the limbic
   system?

9.                                          A: This is called the Kluver-Bucy syndrome.

10. What is the key structure in animals who display Kluver-
    Bucy syndrome?

11. What is the key difference between the James-Lange
    and Cannon-Bard theories in terms of the role of the
    ANS in emotion?

12.                                          A: This is called polygraphy.

13. Why is it difficult to evaluate the effectiveness of
    polygraphy.

14. What is the difference between the control-question
    technique and the guilty-knowledge technique of
    polygraphy?

15. Are facial expressions innate or learned? Defend your
    answer with one piece of experimental evidence.

16.                                          A: These include anger, surprise, sadness, disgust, fear, happiness.

17. What is the facial feedback hypothesis of emotion?

18.                                          A: These are called microexpressions.

19. What is a Duchenne smile?

20.                                          A: These are the zygomaticus major and obicularis oculi muscles.

21. Why is the facial EMG such a sensitive measure of emotion?

22.                                          A: This area in the frontal lobe plays an important role in emotions.

23. Describe some of the evidence that the right hemisphere is the dominant hemisphere for emotion.

24.                                          A: This is called prosody.

25.                                          A: This suggests that laterality of emotion is not unique to humans.

26.                                          A: This is called fear.

27. What is the difference between aggressive behavior and
    defensive behavior?

28.                                        A:  This is called ethoexperimental research.

29.                                        A:  These are called alpha males.

30. What are the 3 general criteria that have been used to
    describe the aggressive and defensive behaviors of rats?

31.                                        A:  This is called the *target-site concept.*

32. Why is the term "septal rage" misleading?

33. Describe the data supporting the idea that human
    aggression is independent of testosterone.

34.                                        A:  This is called the amygdala.

35. Describe the role of the amygdala in fear conditioning.

36.                                        A:  This is a side effect of amygdalectomy.

37.                                        A:  This is called stress.

38. Describe the dual nature of the stress response.

39.                                          A:  This is called the anterior-pituitary-adrenal-cortex system.

40.                                          A:  These are called glucocorticoids.

41. Which two physiological systems play key roles in the stress response?

42. What determines the magnitude of a stress response.

43. What is a psychosomatic illness?

44. How does stress exacerbate the formation of gastric ulcers?

45. Describe the role of *Helicobacter pylori* in the development of ulcers.

46.                                          A:  This field is called psychoneuroimmunology.

47. Describe the two types of immune reactions that might be elicited by a foreign microorganism in the body.

48.                                          A:  These are called antigens.

49. What is phagocytosis?

50. What is the difference between cell-mediated immunity and antibody-mediated immunity?

51. How does stress disrupt immune function?

52. What 3 general conclusions can be reached about the relationship between stress and the immune system?

53. Why does early handling of rat pups reduce their glucocorticoid levels later in life?

54. How does stress affect the cells of the hippocampus?

55. Describe the diathesis-stress model of psychiatric illness.

56.                                         A: This is called schizophrenia.

57. List the symptoms of schizophrenia.

58. What evidence suggests that genetic factors influence schizophrenia?

59. What evidence suggests that stress plays a role in the activation of schizophrenic symptoms?

60.                                          A: This drug is called chlorpromazine.

61. Describe the common antischizophrenic effects of chlorpromazine and reserpine.

62. Describe the dopamine theory of schizophrenia.

63. How does chlorpromazine influence dopamine transmission?

64.                                          A: This drug is called haloperidol.

65. What is a false transmitter?

66. What is the key difference between phenothiazine and butyrophenone antipsychotic drugs?

67. What is unusual about the mechanism of action of clozapine?

68. Describe the depolarization-block hypothesis of antipsychotic drug action.

69. What parts of the brain are involved in schizophrenia?

70. Describe the difference between *positive* and *negative* symptoms of schizophrenia.

71. How does stress exacerbate the symptoms of schizophrenia?

72. What are the two types of affective illness?

73. What is the difference between reactive and endogenous depression?

74. Describe the evidence for the hypothesis that genetics plays a key role in the development of affective disorders.

75.                                                 A:  This drug is called iproniazid.

76. What is a MAO inhibitor?

77. Describe the cheese effect.

78. What is the mechanism of action of imipramine and other tricyclic antidepressants?

79.                                          A: This drug is called lithium.

80. Why was the medical community so slow to accept Cade's claim that lithium was an effective treatment for mania?

81. How does Prozac exert its psychoactive effects?

82. Describe the monoamine hypothesis of depression.

83.                                          A: This is called "up-regulation" of receptors.

84. Describe the hypothalamic-pituitary-adrenal theory of depression.

85. How does stress affect the symptoms of depression?

86. What are the weaknesses of the monoamine theory of depression?

87. What are the symptoms of anxiety?

88. What are the four major classes of anxiety disorders?

89.                                          A: These drugs include Librium and Valium.

90. What is the mechanism of action for the
    benzodiazepines?

91.                                          A: This drug is called buspirone.

92. What is the anxiolytic mechanism of action of
    buspirone?

93. What is the elevated-plus maze test?

94.                                          A: This is called conditioned defensive burying.

95. What brain structure is believed to play a key role in
    anxiety disorders?

Once you have completed the jeopardy study items, study them. Practice bidirectional studying; make sure
that you know the correct answer to every question and the correct question for every answer.

## II.    Essay Study Questions

*Using Chapter 17 of BIOPSYCHOLOGY, write an outline of the answer to each of the following essay study questions.*

1.  Discuss the idea that emotional expression is related to emotional experience.

2.  How does Darwin's theory of the evolution of emotion account for the evolution of threat displays in animals?

3.  According to the pop-science industry, emotion resides in the right hemisphere. Discuss the scientific evidence relevant to this claim.

4. Compare and contrast the monoamine hypothesis of depression and the hypothalamic-pituitary-adrenal hypothesis of depression.

5. What is psychoneuroimmunology? Discuss some of the recent research on the effects of stress on psychoneuroimmunologic function.

6. What is an ethoexperimental approach to research? Describe two examples.

7.  Describe the role of the amygdala in the emotion of fear and in conditioned fear.  Include the possible clinical efficacy of amygdalectomy in humans

8.  Describe the dopamine hypothesis of schizophrenia.  What are the shortcomings of this idea?

9.  Compare and contrast the James-Lange theory of emotion and the Canon-Bard theory of emotion.  Which theory is supported by Eckman's work on facial expressions and emotions?

---

When you have answered the essay study questions, memorize your outlines to  prepare for your upcoming examination.

## III. Practice Examination

*After completing most of your studying of Chapter 17, but at least 24 hours before your formal examination, write the following practice examination.*

**A. Multiple-Choice Section.** Circle the correct answer for each question; *REMEMBER that some questions may have more than one correct answer.*

1. Darwin's theory of the evolution of emotion was based upon the idea that:

   a. expressions of emotion evolved from behaviors that indicate what an animal will do next when faced with a particular situation.
   b. the expression of emotion and the activity of the autonomic nervous system are intimately linked.
   c. if expressions of emotion benefit the animal, they will evolve to maximize their communicative function.
   d. opposite messages are signaled by opposite movements and postures.

2. The limbic system includes:

   a. the hippocampus.
   b. the occipital cortex.
   c. the amygdala.
   d. the thalamus.

3. Eckman and his colleagues have found:

   a. that facial expressions are a universal language of emotion.
   b. that you must *feel* an emotion before you can make the appropriate facial expression.
   c. that you can elicit an emotion by making the appropriate facial expression.
   d. that there are just six primary emotions.

4. The emotional response to threat is called:

   a. stress.
   b. anxiety.
   c. fear.
   d. mania.

5. According to Albert and his colleagues, the failure to find a consistent correlation between human aggression and testosterone levels is due to the fact that:

   a. human aggression is heavily socialized.
   b. researchers often fail to distinguish between defensive aggression and social aggression.
   c. human aggression does not decline in castrated males.
   d. aggression increases testosterone levels, and not the other way around.

6. Auditory fear conditioning depends upon direct or indirect neural pathways from the:

   a. medial geniculate nucleus of the thalamus to primary auditory cortex.
   b. from the ear to the medial geniculate nucleus of the thalamus.
   c. from the medial geniculate nucleus of the thalamus to the amygdala.
   d. from the amygdala to the primary auditory cortex.

7. Selye's conceptualization of the stress response:

    a. marked a key link between psychological and physiological well-being.
    b. focused on activation of the sympathetic nervous system.
    c. focused on activation of the anterior pituitary adrenal cortex system.
    d. emphasized the effects of both acute and chronic stress on an organism.

8. Glucocorticoids are released by the:

    a. adrenal cortex.
    b. adrenal medulla
    c. neocortex.
    d. anterior pituitary.

9. Stress-induced alterations in the function of the immune system are:

    a. clinically significant, although demonstrating this link has been difficult.
    b. likely related to corticosterone or norepinephrine-induced alterations in T-cell and B-cell activity.
    c. observable in laboratory animals as well as human beings.
    d. due to inoculation of stressed individuals.

10. The symptoms of schizophrenia include:

    a. low self-esteem, despair, and suicide.
    b. delusions, hallucinations, odd behavior, incoherent thought, and inappropriate affect.
    c. fear that persists in the absence of any direct threat.
    d. tachycardia, hypertension, and high corticosteroid levels.

11. The monoamine hypothesis of affective illness::

    a. posits that depressed patients have decreased monoaminergic activity and manic patients have increased monoaminergic activity in the CNS.
    b. is compromised by the fact that antidepressants immediately increase central monoamine levels, but the therapeutic effect does not appear for several weeks.
    c. is based on the observation that lithium is not an effective antidepressant.
    d. is supported by the observation that amphetamine and cocaine do not have an antidepressant effect.

12. Pharmacological evidence supports the idea that anxiety is due to deficits in:

    a. corticosteroid activity.
    b. GABAergic activity.
    c. pituitary activity.
    d. serotonergic activity.

13. Anxiolytic drugs like Valium and Librium are:

    a. widely prescribed antipsychotic drugs.
    b. believed to alter neural function by their agonistic action at GABA-A receptors.
    c. prescribed for their hypnotic, anticonvulsant, and muscle relaxant properties.
    d. benzodiazepines.

**B. Modified True-False and Fill-in-the Blank Section.** If the statement is true, write TRUE in the blank provided. If the statement is false, write FALSE as well as the word or words that will make the statement true if they replaced the highlighted word or words in the original statement. If the statement is incomplete, write the word or words that will complete it.

1. According to Darwin, expressions of emotion evolve from behaviors that indicate what an animal is

   _____.

2. According to Darwin's principle of _____, opposite messages are often signaled by opposite movements and postures.

3. Next to each of the following descriptions, write J-L (James-Lange) or C-B (Cannon-Bard).

   a. _____        The first major physiological theory of emotion; proposed in 1884.

   b. _____        The experience of emotion results from the brain's perception of the body's reaction to emotional stimuli.

   c. _____        Emotional expression and emotional experience are parallel processes that have not direct causal relation.

4. **True or False:** The study of sham rage in decerebrate animals implicated the **hypothalmus** in aggressive behavior.

   **A:** _____

5. When considered together, the amygdala, hippocampus, septum, fornix, olfactory bulb, mammillary body, and cingulate cortex are considered to make up the _____.

6. Bilateral destruction of the anterior portions of the temporal lobes often results in a condition called

   _____ syndrome.

7. **True or False:** Enlarged adrenal glands, gastric ulcers, and suppressed immune function are generally caused by exposure to **acute stress.**

   **A:** _____

8. _____ is a method of interrogation in which autonomic nervous system indices of emotion are used to infer the truthfulness of a subject's responses.

9. The most effective polygraphic technique is the _____ technique.

10. According to Eckman and Friesen (1975), the facial expressions of anger, fear, happiness, surprise, sadness, and disgust are called _____.

11. Movement of the _____ _____ muscle distinguishes fake smiles from genuine smiles.

12. Although it is often portrayed as such, it is a mistake to think of emotion as a single global faculty that resides in the _____ hemisphere of the human brain.

13. Gastric ulcers are believed to be caused by an interaction between _____ bacteria and stress-related changes in the flow of blood and the release of hydrochloric acid in the stomach.

14. The lymphocytes that respond specifically to combat particular kinds of invading microorganisms are called _____.

15. When they bind to a foreign antigen, B cells multiply and begin to manufacture _____.

16. The study of the interactions among psychological factors, the nervous system, and the immune system is called _____.

17. Next to each of the following write "alpha male" or "male intruder."

    a.    Piloerection: _____

    b.    Lateral attack: _____

    c.    Boxing: _____

    d.    Back biting: _____

18. **True or False:** The elevated plus maze is used to assess the **antidepressant** effects of drugs.

        **A:** _____

19. Chlorpromazine is a _____ transmitter at dopamine synapses.

20. Both phenothiazines and butyrophenones induce _____-like side effects.

21. The effectiveness of clozapine has implicated _____ receptors in schizophrenia.

22. The first tricyclic antidepressant was _____.

23. Next to each of the following drugs write the psychological disorder that it is effective against.

a. Lithium: _____        f. Reserpine: _____

b. Chlorpromazine: _____        g. Buspirone: _____

c. Iproniazid: _____        h. Clozapine: _____

d. Benzodiazepines: _____        i. Imipramine: _____

e. Haloperidol: _____

## C. Diagrams.

**Figure 1.** Identify the structures of the limbic system.

A) _____

B) _____

C) _____

D) _____

E) _____

F) _____

G) _____

H) _____

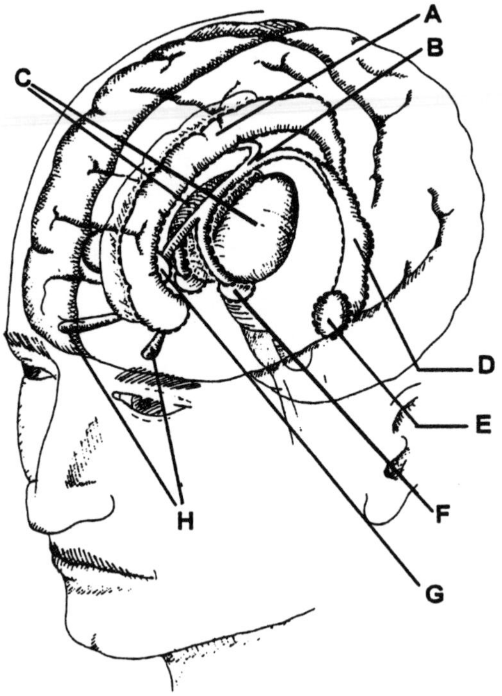

**Figure 2.** Identify the structures that are thought to mediate the sympathetic and behavioral responses to conditioned fear.

A) _____

B) _____

C) _____

D) _____

E) _____

F) _____

G) _____

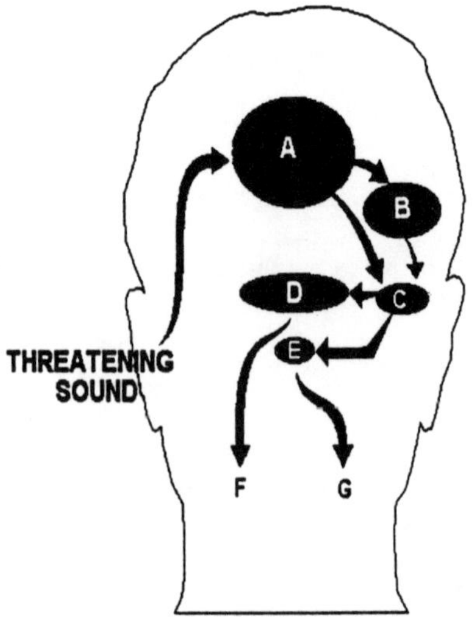

306

**D. Short Answer Section.  In no more than 5 sentences, answer each of the following questions.**

1.  Summarize research that has examined the relationship between facial expression and emotions.

2.  How does stress affect the symptomatology of schizophrenia and affective illness?

3. Comment on the statement "Human aggression is not related to testosterone levels."

4. How are the pharmacological treatments of schizophrenia and depression similar? How do they differ?

5. Discuss evidence that supports the hypothesis that anxiety is mediated by GABAergic mechanisms

**Mark your answers to the practice examination; the correct answers follow. On the basis of your performance, plan the final stages of your studying.**

# Answers to Practice Examination

## A. Multiple Choice Section

| | | |
|---|---|---|
| 1. a, c, d | 6. a, b, c | 11. a, b |
| 2. a, c | 7. a, c, d | 12. b, d |
| 3. a, c, d | 8. a | 13. b, c, d |
| 4. c | 9. a, b, c | |
| 5. b | 10. b | |

## B. Modified True/False and Fill-in-the-Blank Section

1. likely to do next.
2. antithesis
3. a. J-L
   b. J-L
   c. C-B
4. True
5. limbic system
6. Kluver-Bucy
7. False; chronic stress
8. polygraphy
9. guilty-knowledge
10. primary emotions
11. obicularis oculi

12. right
13. *Helicobacter pylori*
14. T-cells
15. antibodies
16. psychoneuroimmunology
17. a. alpha male
    b. alpha male
    c. male intruder
    d. alpha male
18. False; anxiolytic (or antianxiety)
19. false
20. parkinsonian

21. D1; D4; Serotonin
22. imipramine
23. a. bipolar affective disorder
    b. schizophrenia
    c. unipolar affective disorder (or depression)
    d. anxiety disorder
    e. schizophrenia
    f. schizophrenia
    g. anxiety disorder
    h. schizophrenia
    i. unipolar affective disorder (or depression)

## C. Diagrams

**Figure 1.** A) Cingulate Cortex  B) Fornix  C) Thalamus  D) Hippocampus  E) Amygdala
F) Mammillary Body  G) Septum  H) Olfactory Nerves

**Figure 2.** A) Medial Geniculate of Thalamus  B) Auditory Cortex  C) Amygdala  D) Hypothalamus
E) Periaqueductal Gray  F) Sympathetic Response  G) Behavioral Response

## D. Short Answer Section

1. Mention the universality of facial expression and emotion; the six primary facial expressions; the facial feedback hypothesis; and the possibility of voluntary control over facial expression and emotion.

2. Mention that stress often exacerbates the symptoms of schizophrenia; that stress may allow the expression of a genetic predisposition for schizophrenia; that stress may activate the symptoms of schizophrenia due to abnormal development of prefrontal cortex.

3. Mention link between social aggression and testosterone in nonhuman species; that human evidence seems to suggest that there is no relationship between aggression and testosterone, but this may reflect a misguided focus on defensive aggression rather than social aggression.

4. Mention that both types of drugs affect monoaminergic systems and that there is a "startup" period for both drug effects; however, antipsychotics *block* neurotransmission in dopaminergic systems whereas antidepressants *increase* neurotransmission in noradrenergic and serotonergic systems.

5. Mention that many antianxiety drugs alter GABA-A activity; that the amygdala, a key neural structure in anxiety, is high in GABA-A receptors; however, note that the effectiveness of drugs like buspirone suggest that serotonergic activity is involved as well.

# NOTES

# NOTES

# NOTES

# NOTES

# NOTES

# NOTES

# NOTES